ATLAS
OF
BRITISH HISTORY

G.S.P. FREEMAN–GRENVILLE

Cartography Lorraine Kessel

REX COLLINGS LONDON 1979

First published by Rex Collings Ltd.
69 Marylebone High Street, London W1
& produced by Carta Ltd.

This book is available as a Hardback
and Paperback edition.

PREFACE

This atlas aims to provide the general reader and the student with maps of the principal themes and events in the history of the British Isles from prehistoric times until 1978. Its object is to relate their political, social and economic history to its physical setting, rivers, lowlands, hills and mountains, the nearness of the sea and the incidence of mineral wealth, which throughout this long period have been among the determinants of the country's fortunes. It would be mistaken to omit earlier times to make more space for later: Britain had already begun to exploit her mineral wealth for herself before the Romans came: in their turn they developed much of the present road system: the local government administration, radically revised in England and Wales in 1972, and in Scotland in 1973, has pre-Norman bases, some of which survive: the system of royal courts, developed as assizes under the Plantagenets, was revised only in 1973: the same physical system determined the siting of towns, castles and monasteries as determined the industrial revolution and the growth of later industry. The discovery of gas and oil in the sea expands that pattern. One cannot treat the fortunes of the British Isles geographically or historically without reference to Europe, to the former Empire or to the present Commonwealth, or to wars, whether European or global, in which the country has been engaged.

It is necessary to remark especially on maps 3 to 6, which show the state of knowledge of prehistory as it was early in 1976. The exceptional drought of that summer revealed no less than 600 hitherto unrecorded prehistoric sites in Scotland, and more in England. It will of course be some time before so many sites can be accurately assessed or dated.

I forebear to mention all those to whom I owe a debt of gratitude for advice or assistance: they have my warmest thanks, and will, I am sure, forgive the omission of what would be far too long a catalogue of names.

Sheriff Hutton
York

G.S.P.F.–G.

CONTENTS

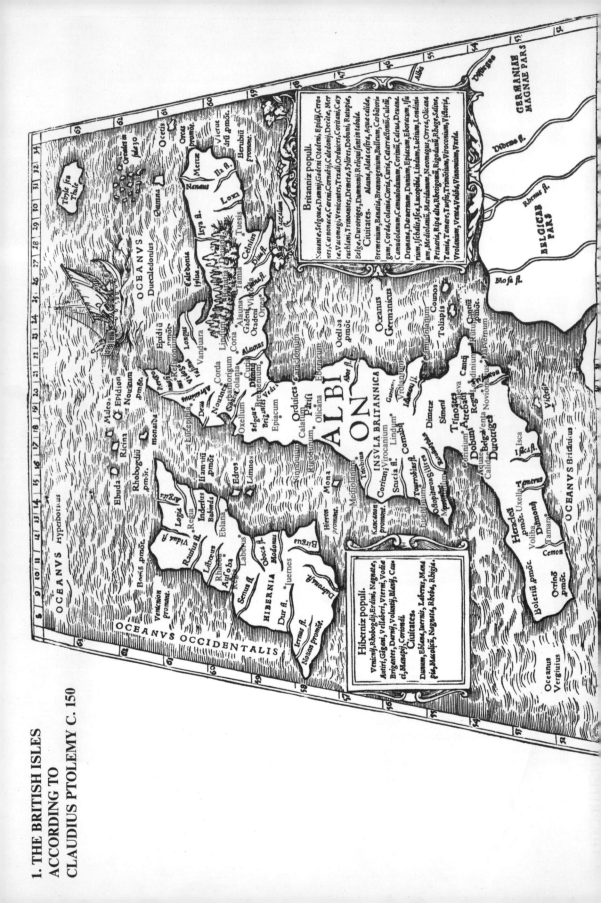

1. THE BRITISH ISLES ACCORDING TO CLAUDIUS PTOLEMY C. 150

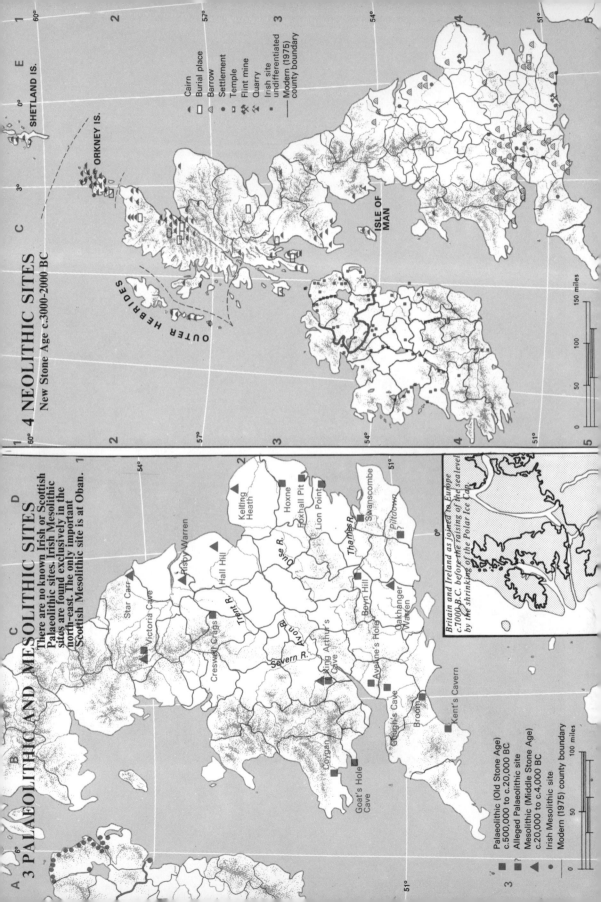

3 PALAEOLITHIC AND MESOLITHIC SITES

There are no known Irish or Scottish Palaeolithic sites. Irish Mesolithic sites are found exclusively in the north-east. The only important Scottish Mesolithic site is at Oban.

Star Carr
Victoria Cave
Creswell Crags
Risby Warren
Hall Hill
Kelling Heath
Hoxne
Foxhall Pit
Lion Point
Swanscombe
Piltdown?
Beyn Hill
Oakhanger Warren
Aveline's Hole
King Arthur's Cave
Gough's Cave
Broom
Kent's Cavern
Goat's Hole Cave
Coygan

Trent R.
Ouse R.
Thames R.
Avon R.
Severn R.

- ■ Palaeolithic (Old Stone Age) c.500,000 to c.20,000 BC
- ■? Alleged Palaeolithic site
- ◀ Mesolithic (Middle Stone Age) c.20,000 to c.4,000 BC
- ● Irish Mesolithic site
- — Modern (1975) county boundary

0   50   100 miles

Britain and Ireland as joined to Europe c.7000 B.C. before the raising of the sea-level by the shrinking of the Polar Ice Cap.

4 NEOLITHIC SITES

New Stone Age c.3000–2000 BC

SHETLAND IS.
ORKNEY IS.
OUTER HEBRIDES
ISLE OF MAN

- ◀ Cairn
- ▭ Burial place
- △ Barrow
- ● Settlement
- ▭ Temple
- ✸ Flint mine
- ✕ Quarry
- ■ Irish site undifferentiated
- — Modern (1975) county boundary

0   50   100   150 miles

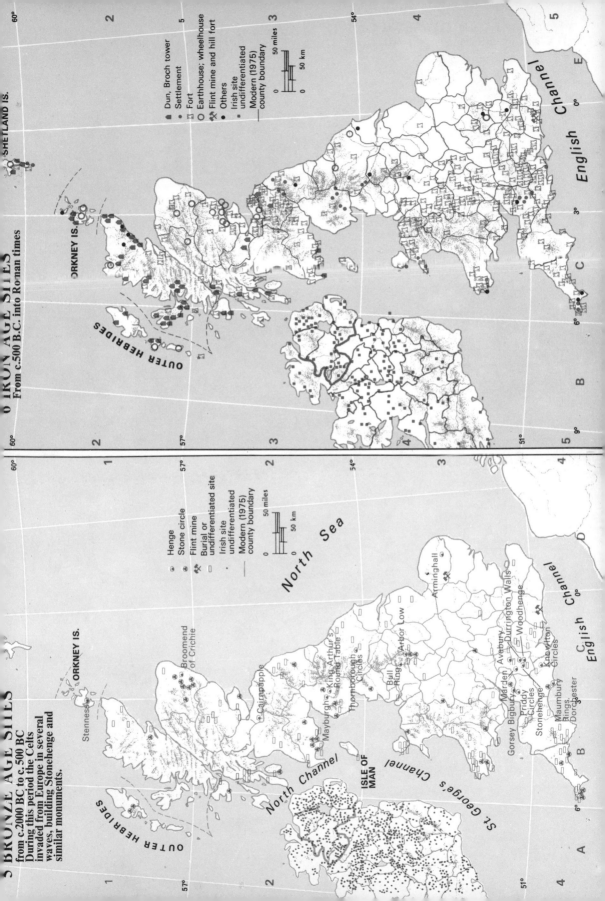

5 BRONZE AGE SITES
from c.2000 BC to c.500 BC
During this period the Celts invaded from Europe in several waves, building Stonehenge and similar monuments.

6 IRON AGE SITES
From c.500 B.C. into Roman times

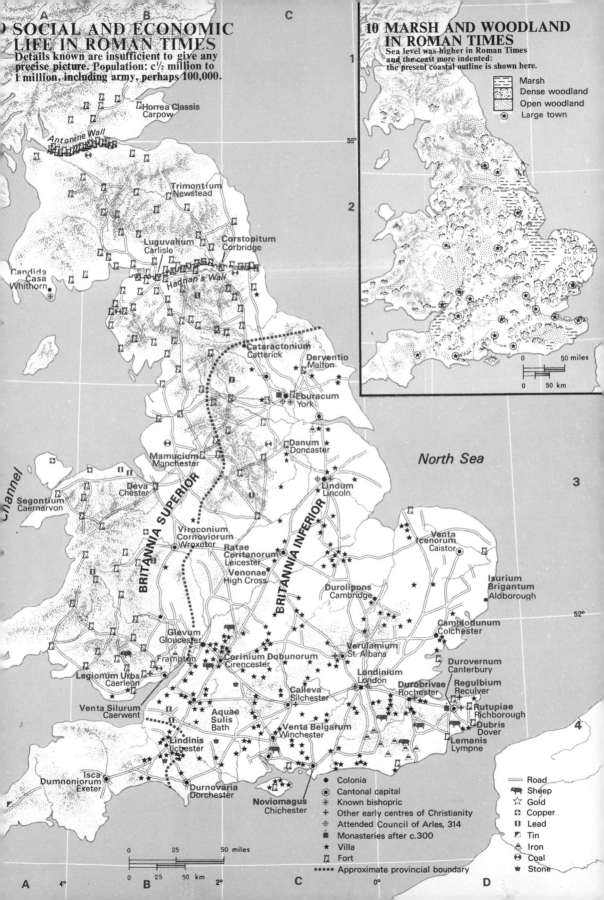

SOCIAL AND ECONOMIC LIFE IN ROMAN TIMES

Details known are insufficient to give any precise picture. Population: c½ million to 1 million, including army, perhaps 100,000.

10 MARSH AND WOODLAND IN ROMAN TIMES

Sea level was higher in Roman Times and the coast more indented: the present coastal outline is shown here.

Marsh
Dense woodland
Open woodland
⊛ Large town

0   50 miles
0   50 km

Horrea Classis
Carpow

Antonine Wall

56°

Trimontium
Newstead

Candida
Casa
Whithorn

Luguvalium
Carlisle

Corstopitum
Corbridge

Hadrian's Wall

Cataractonium
Catterick

Derventio
Malton

Eburacum
York

North Sea

3

Danum
Doncaster

Mamucium
Manchester

BRITANNIA SUPERIOR

Deva
Chester

Lindum
Lincoln

Segontium
Caernarvon

Viroconium
Cornoviorum
Wroxeter

Venta
Icenorum
Caistor

Channel

Ratae
Coritanorum
Leicester

BRITANNIA INFERIOR

Isurium
Brigantum
Aldborough

Venonae
High Cross

52°

Durolipons
Cambridge

Glevum
Gloucester

Camulodunum
Colchester

Frampton

Corinium Dobunorum
Cirencester

Verulamium
St. Albans

Durovernum
Canterbury

Legionium Urbs
Caerleon

Londinium
London

Durobrivae
Rochester

Regulbium
Reculver

Venta Silurum
Caerwent

Calleva
Silchester

Rutupiae
Richborough

Aquae
Sulis
Bath

Venta Belgarum
Winchester

Dubris
Dover

Lindinis
Ilchester

Lemanis
Lympne

4

Isca
Dumnoniorum
Exeter

Durnovaria
Dorchester

Noviomagus
Chichester

● Colonia
◉ Cantonal capital
✙ Known bishopric
✛ Other early centres of Christianity
⊕ Attended Council of Arles, 314
■ Monasteries after c.300
★ Villa
⌂ Fort
⋯ Approximate provincial boundary

═ Road
🐑 Sheep
☆ Gold
⊡ Copper
Ⅱ Lead
◩ Tin
△ Iron
✦ Coal
⚒ Stone

0   25   50 miles
0   25   50 km

A   4°   B   2°   C   0°   D

11 BRITAIN AND ITS INVADERS, 4TH TO 5TH CENTURIES

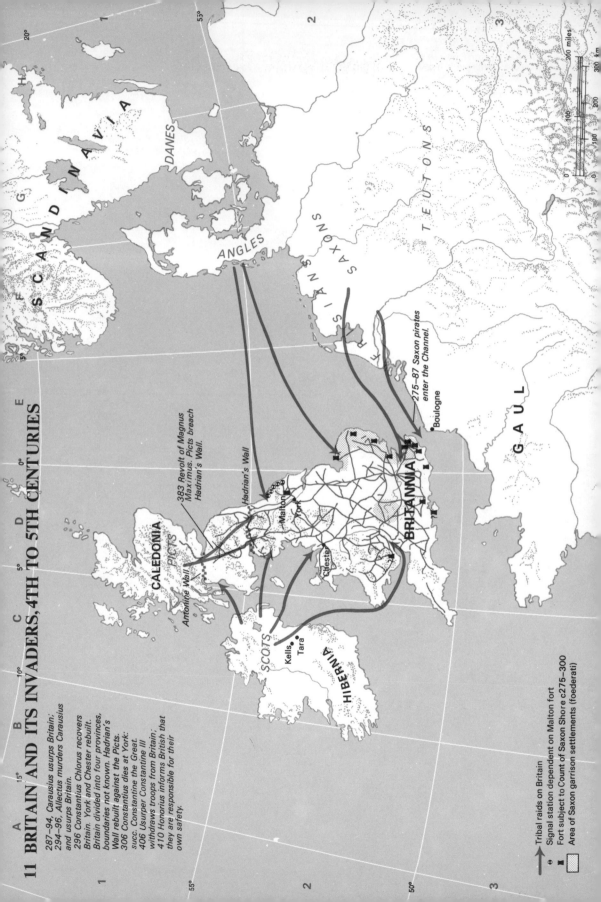

287–94, Carausius usurps Britain;
294–96, Allectus murders Carausius
and usurps Britain.
296 Constantius Chlorus recovers
Britain. York and Chester rebuilt.
Britain divided into four provinces,
boundaries not known. Hadrian's
Wall rebuilt against the Picts.
306 Constantius dies at York:
succ. Constantine the Great.
406 Usurper Constantine III
withdraws troops from Britain;
410 Honorius informs British that
they are responsible for their
own safety.

383 Revolt of Magnus
Maximus. Picts breach
Hadrian's Wall.

Hadrian's Wall

275–87 Saxon pirates
enter the Channel.

Boulogne

Antonine Wall

CALEDONIA

PICTS

Malton

York

Chester

BRITANNIA

Kells

Tara

HIBERNIA

SCOTS

ANGLES

SAXONS

FRISIANS

TEUTONS

DANES

SCANDINAVIA

GAUL

→ Tribal raids on Britain
Signal station dependent on Malton fort
Fort subject to Count of Saxon Shore c275–300
Area of Saxon garrison settlements (foederati)

0   100   200   300 Km
0   100   200 miles

12 CHRISTIANITY IN IRELAND 4TH TO 9TH CENTURIES

13 CHRISTIANITY IN SCOTLAND, 4TH TO 9TH CENTURIES

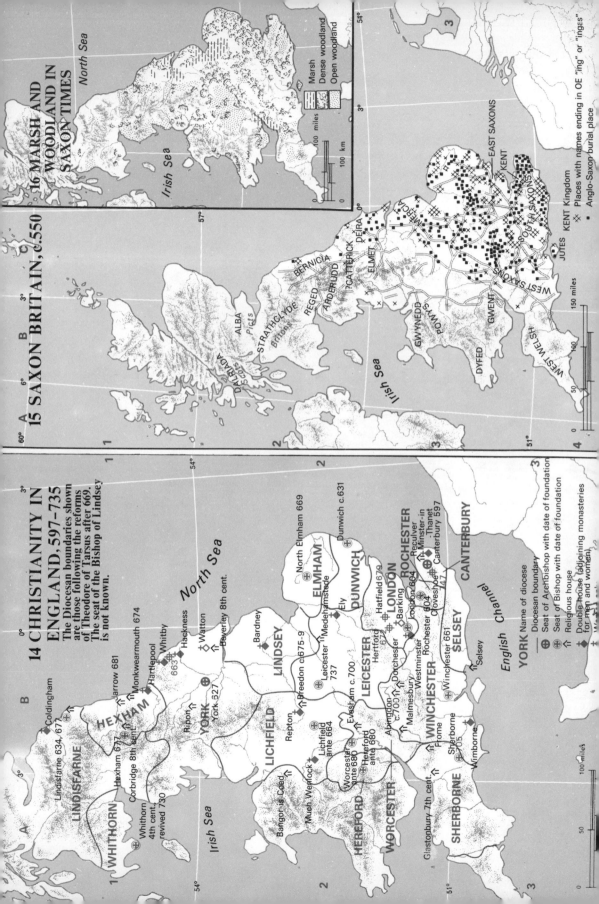

14 CHRISTIANITY IN ENGLAND, 597-735

15 SAXON BRITAIN, c.550

16 MARSH AND WOODLAND IN SAXON TIMES

THE GROWTH OF WESSEX, c.495-829

CILTERN SAETE
Ellundun
Dyrham ✕
EAST SEAXE
Bristol Channel
WILTSAETE
Galford
Kingston
DEFNAS
DORNSAETE
SUTHRIGE
CANTWARE
WALES
SUTH SAXE
WIHT WARE

Nucleus conquered under Cerdic and Cynric, c.495-560
Conquests of Ceawlin (c.560-92), but not finally held till later
Probable expansion c.652-82
Probable expansion c.650-70
Further conquests c.685-726
Further conquests, probably 8th cent.
Conquered by Egbert, 825-29
✕ Battle

50 miles
0   50 km

18 ENGLAND AND WALES, c.600

0   50 miles
0   50 km

STRATHCLYDE
BERNICIA
PICTS
?REGED
NORTHUMBRIA
DEIRA
ELMET
GWYNEDD
POWYS
MERCIA
MIDDLE ANGLES
EAST ANGLES
DYFED
GWENT
HWICCE
WESSEX
ESSEX
WEST WELSH
SUSSEX
KENT

Kingdom of Ethelbert of Kent
Kingdoms subject to Ethelbert of Kent
ELMET Kingdom

SUPREMACY OF EDWIN OF NORTHUMBERLAND, 617-32

STRATHCLYDE
BERNICIA
PICTS
NORTHUMBRIA
CUMBRIA
DEIRA
GWYNEDD
POWYS
MERCIA
MIDDLE ANGLES
EAST ANGLES
DYFED
GWENT
HWICCE
WESSEX
ESSEX
KENT
WEST WELSH
SUSSEX
JUTES

0   50 miles
0   50 km

Kingdom of Edwin
Under the overlordship of Edwin
Boundaries of kingdoms mentioned by the Venerable Bede

20 SUPREMACY OF PENDA OF MERCIA, 626-55

STRATHCLYDE
BERNICIA
PICTS
CUMBRIA
GWYNEDD
MERCIA
POWYS
EAST ANGLES
DYFED
HWICCE
WESSEX
ESSEX
GWENT
KENT
WEST WELSH
SUSSEX
JUTES

Penda's kingdom
Probable extent of Mercian supremacy

0   50 miles
0   50 km

21 SUPREMACY OF OSWY OF NORTHUMBERLAND, 655-58

STRATHCLYDE
BERNICIA
PICTS
NORTHUMBRIA
DEIRA
ELMET
LINDSEY
GWYNEDD
NORTH MERCIANS
POWYS
SOUTH MERCIANS
MIDDLE ANGLES
DYFED
HWICCE
GWENT
WESSEX
WEST WELSH
SUSSEX
KENT
JUTES

0   50 miles
0   50 km

Oswy's kingdom
Under overlordship of Oswy
Other boundaries

22 SUPREMACIES OF OSWY OF NORTHUMBERLAND AND WULFHERE OF MERCIA, 664

BERNICIA
PICTS
NORTHUMBRIA
DEIRA
GWYNEDD
MERCIA
LINDSEY
POWYS
SOUTH MERCIANS
MIDDLE ANGLES
EAST ANGLES
DYFED
HWICCE
GWENT
WESSEX
ESSEX
WEST WELSH
SUSSEX
KENT
WEST SAXONS
JUTES

0   50 miles
0   50 km

Kingdom of Oswy of Northumberland
Kingdom of Wulfhere of Mercia
Extent of overlordship of Oswy
Extent of overlordship of Wulfhere
– – – Other boundaries

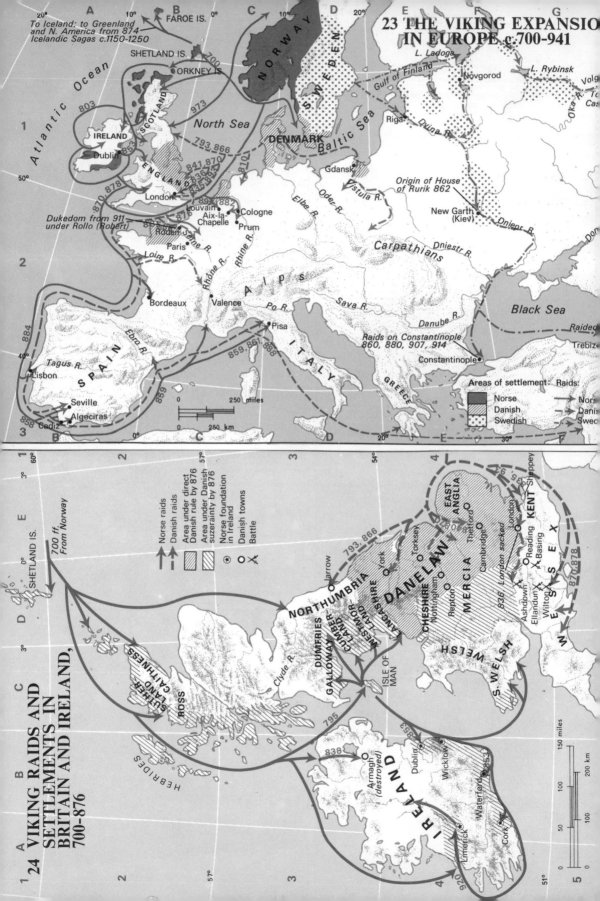

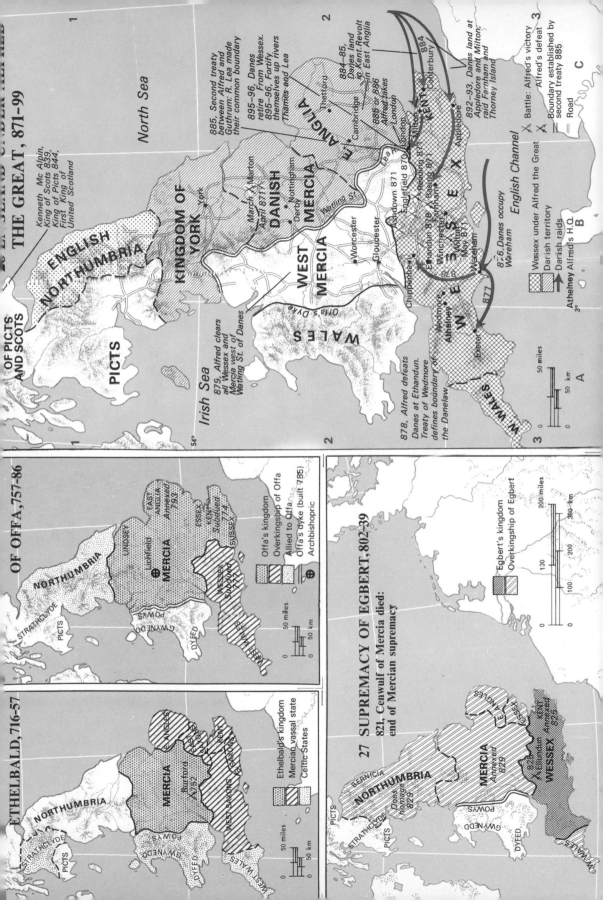

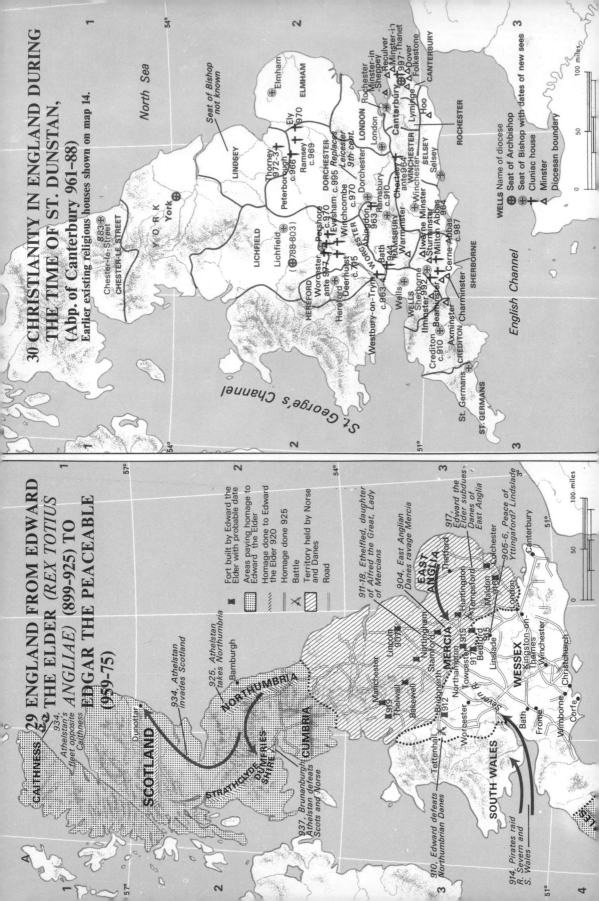

29 ENGLAND FROM EDWARD THE ELDER (REX TOTIUS ANGLIAE) (899–925) TO EDGAR THE PEACEABLE (959–75)

30 CHRISTIANITY IN ENGLAND DURING THE TIME OF ST. DUNSTAN, (Abp. of Canterbury 961–88)
Earlier existing religious houses shown on map 14.

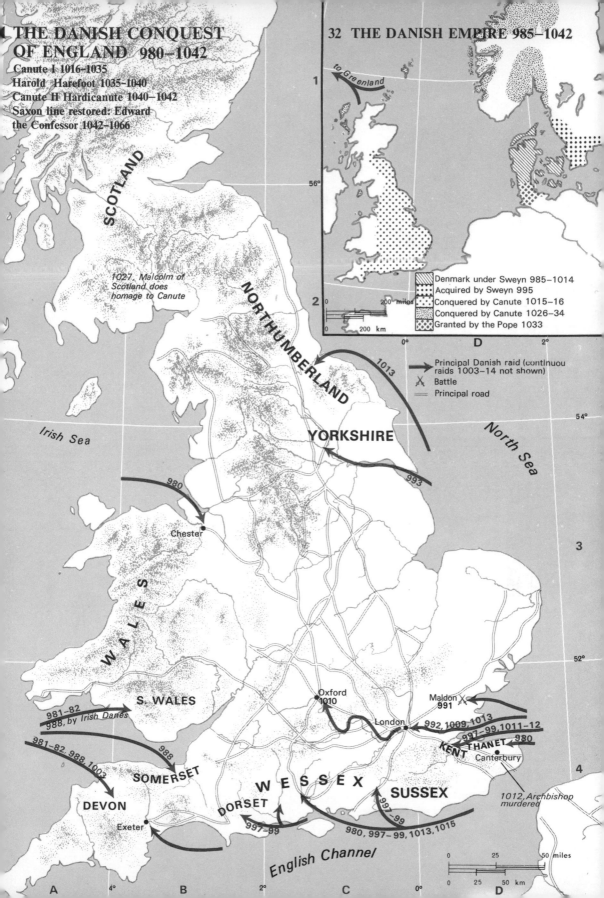

THE DANISH CONQUEST OF ENGLAND 980–1042

Canute I 1016–1035
Harold Harefoot 1035–1040
Canute II Hardicanute 1040–1042
Saxon line restored: Edward
the Confessor 1042–1066

32 THE DANISH EMPIRE 985–1042

to Greenland

Denmark under Sweyn 985–1014
Acquired by Sweyn 995
Conquered by Canute 1015–16
Conquered by Canute 1026–34
Granted by the Pope 1033

Principal Danish raid (continuou
raids 1003–14 not shown)
Battle
Principal road

SCOTLAND

1027, Malcolm of
Scotland does
homage to Canute

NORTHUMBERLAND

Irish Sea

YORKSHIRE

North Sea

1013

993

980

Chester

W A L E S

S. WALES

Oxford
1010

Maldon
991

London

992, 1009, 1013

997–99, 1011–12

997–99, 1011–12

980

KENT

THANET

Canterbury

981–82,
988, by Irish Danes

988

981–82, 988, 1003

SOMERSET

DEVON

Exeter

DORSET

W E S S E X

SUSSEX

1012, Archbishop
murdered

997–99

997–99

980, 997–99, 1013, 1015

English Channel

0   25   50 miles

0   25   50 km

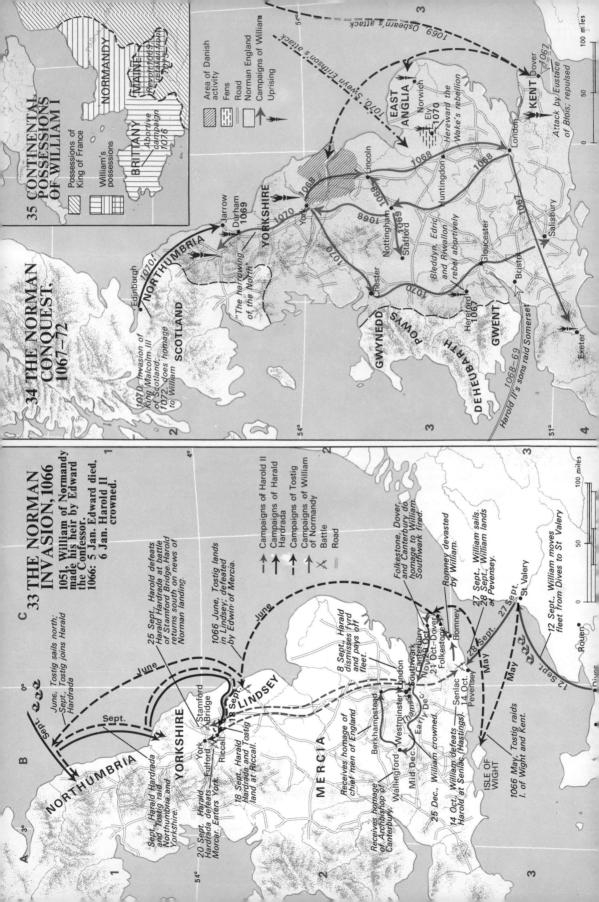

36 THE NORMANS AND WALES, 1068–1200

Irish Sea
Liverpool Bay
GWYNEDD
Chester
CHESTER
St. Asaph
Bangor
Mold
Oswestry
Shrewsbury
SHREWSBURY
POWYS
Welshpool
Montgomery
Clun
Ludlow
Knighton
Cardigan Bay
Aberystwyth
Wye R.
New Radnor
Castle Foel Allt
Builth
Painscastle
HEREFORD
Clifford
Hereford
Kilpeck
Longtown
Monmouth
Cardigan
Lampeter
Llangarth
Brecon
Abergavenny
Raglan
Chepstow
Penhow Castle
DEHEUBARTH
Llandovery
Usk
GWENT
Newport
Narberth
Carmarthen
Kidwelly
Neath
Caerphilly
MORGANWG
Llandaff
Cardiff
St. Davids
Tenby
Manorbier
Swansea
Kenfig
Bridgend
Cowbridge
Milford Haven
Pembroke
Ogmore
Turbervilles
Bristol Channel
Severn R.

1136 Griffith ap Rhys defeats Anglo-Flemish force
Visited by William I, 1081
Henry II receives homage for Wales 1171

GWYNEDD Welsh principality
CHESTER Palatine County instituted by William I
— — — Boundary of Palatine County
━━━ Welsh border
Castles erected following conquest of Robert FitzHamon, Earl of Gloucester
Other castles built before 1200
Cathedral
City

0 20 40 miles
0 20 40 60 km

37 NORMAN ENGLAND IN THE DOMESDAY BOOK, 1086–1087
38 ROYAL FORESTS IN NORMAN ENGLAND

Firth of Forth
Edinburgh
KINGDOM OF SCOTLAND
Newcastle-upon-Tyne
Durham
Lancaster
York
Chester
Lincoln
Nottingham
Derby
Stafford
Shrewsbury
WALES
Hereford
Worcester
Warwick
Gloucester
Leicester
Oakham
Huntingdon
Northampton
Bedford
Cambridge
Bury St Edmunds
Thetford
Norwich
Ipswich
Chelmsford
Witham
Chigwell
Hertford
Aylesbury
Oxford
Bristol
Wells
Taunton
Exeter
Bodmin
Dorchester
Salisbury
Winchester
Devizes
Reading
Kingston-upon-Thames
Guildford
London (The Tower)
Greenwich
Gravesend
Dartford
Maidstone
Sevenoaks
Lewes

1. Bedfordshire
2. Berkshire
3. Buckinghamshire
4. Cambridgeshire
5. Cheshire
6. Cornwall
7. Derbyshire
8. Devonshire
9. Dorsetshire
10. Durham
11. Essex
12. Gloucestershire
13. Hampshire
14. Herefordshire
15. Hertfordshire
16. Huntingdonshire
17. Kent
18. Lancashire
19. Leicestershire
20. Lincolnshire
21. London
22. Middlesex
23. Norfolk
24. Northamptonshire
25. Nottinghamshire
26. Oxfordshire
27. Rutland
28. Shropshire
29. Somerset
30. Staffordshire
31. West Suffolk
32. East Suffolk
33. Surrey
34. East Sussex
35. West Sussex
36. Warwickshire
37. Wiltshire
38. Worcestershire
39. East Riding
40. North Riding
41. West Riding
42. Isle of Man

Marcher earldoms
Area of Domesday Book Vol. I
Area of Domesday Book Vol. II
Royal castle
Principal baronial castle
County boundary
Royal forests
Fenland

0 50 miles
0 50 km

39 THE CHURCH IN BRITAIN, c. 1090–1150

1066: 35 religious houses
1100: 50 abbeys, 29 cells
and 45 alien priories

North Sea

Irish Sea

I R E L A N D

Diocesan boundaries
after the reforms
of Lanfranc (1070–89)
⊕ Archbishopric
▪ Cathedral city
⊕ Councils held by Lanfranc,
with date
⌂ New cathedral
◇ New abbey
⊓ New priory
⌒ Gilbertines
✳ Savigni
⊤ White Canons
✦ Cluny
★ Celtic foundations existing
in or after 1050

Fortrose
Elgin
Monymusk
Brechin
Dunkeld
Monifieth
Inchaffray
Abernethy
Dunblane
Muthill
Leven
St. Andrews
Inchcolm
Iona
Newhouse

Alnwick

*From Chester-
le-Street 994*

Carlisle
1133
Durham
Whithorn
Calder
Jervaulx
Byland
Malton
Rushen
Furness
York
Watton

From Dorchester

*From Lichfield
1075
Removed to
Coventry 1102*
Alvingham
Sixhills
Bullington
Basingwerk
Chester
Lincoln
Kirkstead
Combermere
Newstead
Cattley
Swineshead
Haverholme
Buildwas
Sempringham
Norwich
From Thetford 1
Ely
1109
Coventry
Bury
St. Edmunds
Worcester
Chicksand
Hereford
Gloucester
1081,1085
St.
Albans
Coggeshall
Stratford
Langthorne
Neath
London
1075, 1078
(Westminster
Hall)
Rochester
Stanley
From Wells 1080
Bath
Winchester
1072,
1076
Canterbury
(St. Augustine's)
Old
Sarum
Lewes
Chichester
Battle
*From Crediton
1050*
Exeter
Quarr
From Selsey 1075
Buckfast
*From Sherborne
1075*

C h a n n e l

English

0   50   100 miles
0   50   100   150 km

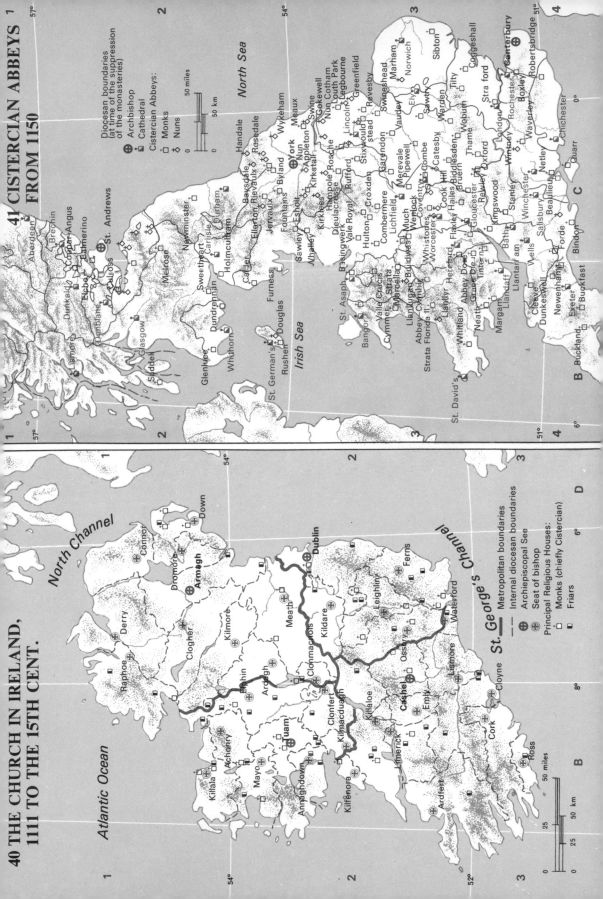

41 CISTERCIAN ABBEYS 1 FROM 1150

Diocesan boundaries (at time of the suppression of the monasteries)
⊕ Archbishop
† Cathedral
Cistercian Abbeys:
□ Monks
◇ Nuns

50 miles

50 km

North Sea

Aberdeen
Brechin
Coupar-Angus
Dunkeld
Camerino
St. Andrews
Elgin
Culross
Dunblane
Lismore
Dunure
Glasgow
Saddell
Glenluce
Whithorn
Dundrennan

Melrose
Sweetheart
Holmcultram
Newminster
Durham
Carter
Baysdale
Rievaulx
Handale
Rosedale
Ellerton
Jervaulx
Fountains
Byland
Wykeham
Meaux
Swine
York
Nun Appleton
Esholt
Kirkstall
Kirklees
Hampole
Rosche
Dieulacresse
Roche
Nun Cotham
Louth Park
Legbourne
Greenfield
Lincoln
Stixwould
Revesby
Marham
Norwich
Sibton
Coggeshall
Canterbury
Rochester
Boxley
Robertsbridge
Chichester

Furness
St. German's
Rushen
Douglas

Irish Sea

St. Asaph
Bangor
Valle Crucis
Cymmer
Abbey-Cwmhir
Strata Florida II
St. David's

Sawley
Whalley
Baingwerk
Hulton
Croxden
Combermere
Lichfield
Much Wenlock
Coventry
Worcester
Whistones
Flaxley
Hereford
Abbey Dore
Grace Dieu
Tintern
Llantarnam
Neath
Margam
Llandaff
Llanllyr
Whitland
Cwm

Strata Marcella
Merevale
Pipewell
Garendon
Vaudey
Elstow
Sawtry
Ely
Warden
Tilty
Thame
Biddlesden
Bruern
Oxford
Rewley
Woburn
London
Waverley
Netley
Winchester
Wells
Beaulieu
Cleeve
Dunkeswell
Newenham
Ford
Exeter
Bindon
Buckland
Buckfast
Quarr

Wombridge
Cook Hill
Hailes
Combe
Catesby
Stanley
Gloucester
Bath
Kingswood
Salisbury

40 THE CHURCH IN IRELAND, 1111 TO THE 15TH CENT.

North Channel

Atlantic Ocean

Connor
Down
Dromore
Armagh
Derry
Raphoe
Clogher
Kilmore
Meath
Kilfala
Achonry
Mayo
Tuam
Annaghdown
Kilmacduagh
Clonfert
Kilfenora
Elphin
Ardagh
Clonmacnois
Kildare
Dublin
Leighlin
Ferns
Killaloe
Ossory
Limerick
Cashel
Lismore
Emly
Ardfert
Cloyne
Cork
Ross

St. George's Channel

— Metropolitan boundaries
- - - Internal diocesan boundaries
⊕ Archiepiscopal See
⊕ Seat of bishop
Principal Religious Houses:
□ Monks (chiefly Cistercian)
□ Friars

50 miles
25   50 km
0   25   50 km

42 THE ANARCHY UNDER STEPHEN 1135-54
Until Matilda's renunciation of the throne, 1152

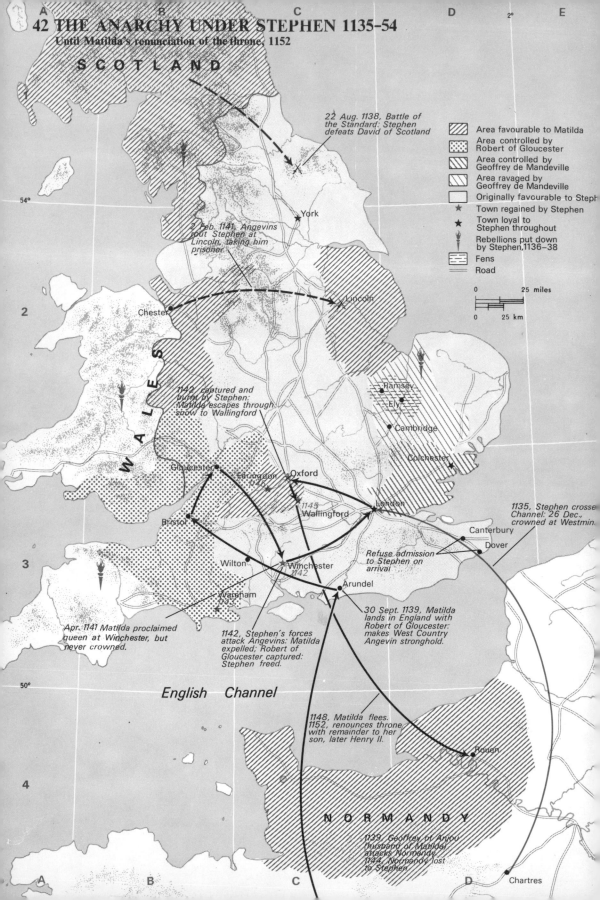

SCOTLAND

22 Aug. 1138, Battle of the Standard: Stephen defeats David of Scotland

York

2 Feb. 1141, Angevins rout Stephen at Lincoln, taking him prisoner.

Chester

Lincoln

1142, captured and burnt by Stephen: Matilda escapes through snow to Wallingford

W A L E S

Ramsey
Ely
Cambridge

Colchester

Gloucester
Faringdon
1145
Oxford
1145
Wallingford
London

Bristol

Wilton
Winchester
1142
Arundel
Canterbury
Dover

1135, Stephen crosses Channel: 26 Dec., crowned at Westmin.

Refuse admission to Stephen on arrival

Wareham
1135

Apr. 1141 Matilda proclaimed queen at Winchester, but never crowned.

1142, Stephen's forces attack Angevins: Matilda expelled; Robert of Gloucester captured: Stephen freed.

30 Sept. 1139, Matilda lands in England with Robert of Gloucester: makes West Country Angevin stronghold.

English Channel

1148, Matilda flees.
1152, renounces throne with remainder to her son, later Henry II.

N O R M A N D Y

Rouen

1139, Geoffrey of Anjou (husband of Matilda) attacks Normandy.
1144, Normandy lost to Stephen.

Chartres

Legend
- Area favourable to Matilda
- Area controlled by Robert of Gloucester
- Area controlled by Geoffrey de Mandeville
- Area ravaged by Geoffrey de Mandeville
- Originally favourable to Steph[en]
- ★ Town regained by Stephen
- ★ Town loyal to Stephen throughout
- Rebellions put down by Stephen,1136–38
- Fens
- Road

0   25 miles
0   25 km

43 THE DOMINIONS OF HENRY II PLANTAGENET. 1154-89

First Plantagenet King.
In popular legend this family
was descended from the Devil

Henry's dominions:

- By cession from his father, 1149
- By succession from his father, 1150
- Dukedoms in the right of his wife, 1152
- By succession in the right of his mother, 1154
- Lands over which Henry claimed suzerainty
- Possessions of King of France
- Vassal dukedom

North Sea

SCOTLAND

IRELAND

Dublin

GWYNEDD

WALES

ENGLAND

London

29 Dec. 1170,
St. Thomas Becket
murdered

1167-71, Invasions
by Henry II or his
vassals

Winchester

Canterbury

Nov. 1153, Stephen
agrees to share
power with Henry

English Channel

1174, William the Lion,
King of Scots, does
homage to Henry
for Scotland

NORMANDY

Paris

Falaise

BRITTANY

MAINE

F R A N C E

ANJOU

Atlantic Ocean

BURGUNDY

POITOU

AQUITAINE

AUVERGNE

HOLY ROMAN EMPIRE

Bordeaux

TOULOUSE

GASCONY

Mediterranean
Sea

SPAIN

0   50   100   150 miles

0   100   200 km

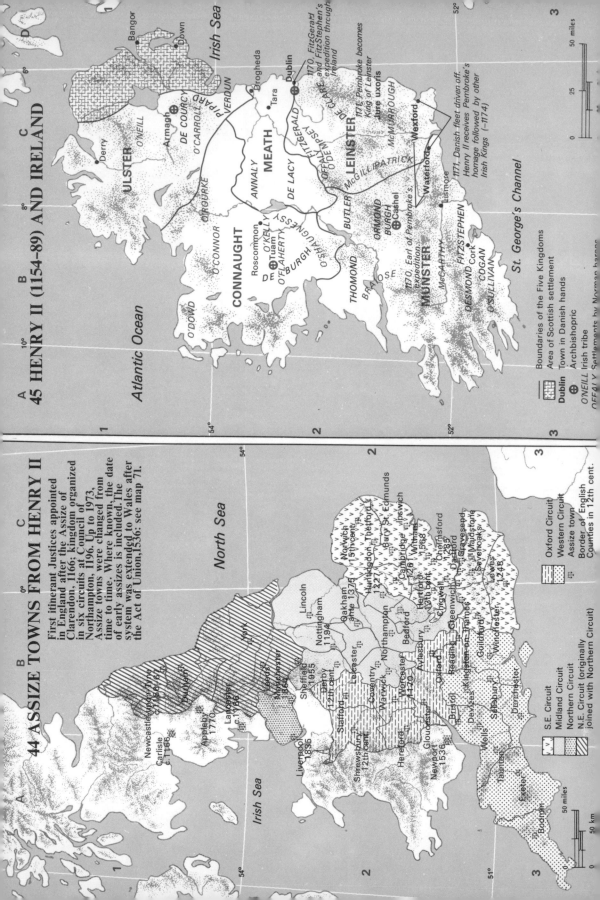

45 HENRY II (1154-89) AND IRELAND

Atlantic Ocean

Irish Sea

St. George's Channel

ULSTER
O'NEILL

Bangor
Down
Derry

Armagh
DE COURCY
O'CARROLL
PIPARD
VERDUN

Drogheda
Tara

MEATH
DE LACY
ANNALY
FITZGERALD
O'DEMPSEY
OFFALY

CONNAUGHT
O'DOWD
O'CONNOR
O'KELLY
DE BURGH
O'FLAHERTY
Roscommon
Tuam
O'SHAUGHNESSY

LEINSTER
BUTLER
McGILLIPATRICK
McMURROUGH

Dublin

1170, FitzGerald and FitzStephen's expedition through Ireland

1171, Pembroke becomes King of Leinster *jure uxoris*

Wexford

1171, Danish fleet driven off.
1171, Pembroke receives homage followed by other Irish Kings (–1174)

Waterford

THOMOND
O'BRIEN
ORMOND
BURGH
Cashel

1170, Earl of Pembroke's expedition

Lismore

MUNSTER
McCARTHY
FITZSTEPHEN
DESMOND
COGAN
O'SULLIVAN
Cork

Boundaries of the Five Kingdoms
Area of Scottish settlement
Town in Danish hands
Dublin Archbishopric
O'NEILL Irish tribe
OFFALY Settlements by Norman barons

0   25   50 miles

---

44 ASSIZE TOWNS FROM HENRY II

First itinerant Justices appointed in England after the Assize of Clarendon, 1166; kingdom organized in six circuits at Council of Northampton, 1176. Up to 1973, Assize towns were changed from time to time. Where known, the date of early assizes is included. The system was extended to Wales after the Act of Union, 1536: see map 71.

North Sea

Irish Sea

Newcastle upon Tyne c.1166/61
Carlisle c.1166
Durham
Appleby 1770
York
Lancaster c.1166
Liverpool 1835
Leeds
Manchester 1864
Sheffield 1955
Lincoln
Nottingham 1194
Derby 12th cent.
Leicester
Stafford
Shrewsbury 12th cent.
Coventry
Warwick
Hereford
Worcester 1170
Gloucester
Newport 1536
Bristol
Wells
Taunton
Exeter
Bodmin
Oakham date 1375
Huntingdon 1327
Northampton
Cambridge 1261
Bedford
Aylesbury
Oxford
Reading
Devizes
Salisbury
Dorchester
Winchester
Kingston-on-Thames
Guildford
Lewes 1248
Maidstone
Sevenoaks
Gravesend
Greenwich 13th cent.
Chigwell
Ilford
Chelmsford
Hertford 13th cent.
Witham 1568
Bury St. Edmunds
Thetford
Ipswich
Norwich 15th cent.

S.E. Circuit
Midland Circuit
Northern Circuit
N.E. Circuit (originally joined with Northern Circuit)
Oxford Circuit
Western Circuit
Assize town
Border of English Counties in 12th cent.

0   50 km
0   50 miles

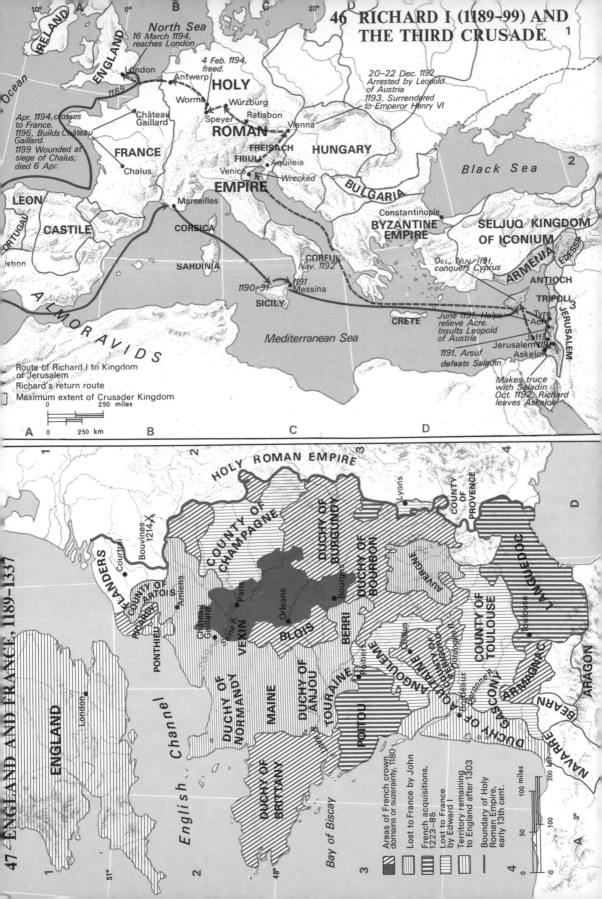

46 RICHARD I (1189-99) AND THE THIRD CRUSADE

North Sea

16 March 1194,
reaches London

4 Feb. 1194,
freed.

London

Antwerp

HOLY

Worms
Würzburg
Speyer
Ratisbon

ROMAN

Château
Gaillard

20-22 Dec. 1192
Arrested by Leopold
of Austria
1193, Surrendered
to Emperor Henry VI

Apr. 1194, crosses
to France.
1196, Builds Château
Gaillard.
1199 Wounded at
siege of Chalus;
died 6 Apr.

1189

ENGLAND

IRELAND

Ocean

FRANCE

Chalus

Vienna

FREISACH
FRIULI

Aquileia

Venice

Wrecked

EMPIRE

HUNGARY

BULGARIA

Black Sea

LEON

CASTILE

PORTUGAL

sbon

Marseilles

CORSICA

SARDINIA

A L M O R A V I D S

Constantinople

**BYZANTINE
EMPIRE**

**SELJUQ KINGDOM
OF ICONIUM**

ARMENIA

EDESSA

CORFU
Nov. 1192

1190-91

Messina

SICILY

*Oct.-Nov 1191,
conquers Cyprus*

ANTIOCH

TRIPOLI

Tyre
Acre

CRETE

June 1191, Helps
relieve Acre.
Insults Leopold
of Austria

1191, Arsuf
defeats Saladin

Jaffa
Jerusalem
Askelon

JERUSALEM

Mediterranean Sea

Makes truce
with Saladin
Oct. 1192. Richard
leaves Askelon

Route of Richard I to Kingdom
of Jerusalem
Richard's return route
Maximum extent of Crusader Kingdom

0   250 miles

0   250 km

47 ENGLAND AND FRANCE, 1189-1337

HOLY ROMAN EMPIRE

Lyons

**COUNTY
OF
PROVENCE**

Bouvines
1214

Courtrai

FLANDERS

**COUNTY OF
CHAMPAGNE**

**DUCHY OF
BURGUNDY**

**DUCHY OF
BOURBON**

AUVERGNE

COUNTY OF
ARTOIS

Amiens

PICARDY

PONTHIEU

Château
Gaillard
Seine R.

Paris

Orleans

Bourges

VEXIN

BLOIS

BERRI

**COUNTY OF
TOULOUSE**

LANGUEDOC

**DUCHY OF
NORMANDY**

MAINE

**DUCHY OF
ANJOU**

TOURAINE

Poitiers

POITOU

Chalus

DUCHY OF
ANGOULÊME

Dordogne R.

Bordeaux
Garonne R.

DUCHY OF
GASCONY

ARMAGNAC

Toulouse

NAVARRE

BEARN

ARAGON

London

ENGLAND

English Channel

**DUCHY OF
BRITTANY**

Bay of Biscay

Areas of French crown
domains or suzerainty, 1180
Lost to France by John
French acquisitions,
1223-85
Lost to France
by Edward I
Territory remaining
to England after 1303
Boundary of Holy
Roman Empire,
early 13th cent.

0   50   100 miles

0   200 km

Royal forests

Principal weaving centr
Monastery supplying w
Cinque port
Town with Jewish quar
Road

Irish Sea

North Sea

English Channel

Southern Uplands
Cheviot Hills
Clyde R.
Nith R.
Tweed R.
Esk R.
Tay R.
Tyne R.
Tees R.
Swale R.
Ure R.
Wharfe R.
Ouse R.
Aire R.
Ribble R.
Mersey R.
Weaver R.
Dee R.
Dove R.
Trent R.
Welland R.
Ouse R.
Yare R.
Waveney R.
Severn R.
Wye R.
Towy R.
Avon R.
Lea R.
Thames R.
Wey R.
Test R.
Itchen R.
Arun R.
Medway R.
Stour R.
Avon R.
Tamar R.
Exe R.
Parrett R.

Pennine Chain
Cambrian Mountains
WALES
Cotswold Hills
Chiltern Hills
North Downs
The Weald
Mendip Hills
Exmoor
Dartmoor

Whitby
Rievaulx
Byland
Jervaulx
Fountains
Furness
York
Beverley
Kirkstall
Hull
Bolton
Lincoln
Nottingham
Leicester
Stamford
Crowland
Lynn
Norwich
Buildwas
Coventry
Huntingdon
Worcester
Warwick
Northampton
Bury St. Edmunds
Bedford
Cambridge
Ipswich
Winchcombe
Sudbury
Colchester
Dore
Gloucester
Oxford
Hertford
Neath
Wallingford
London
Tintern
Bristol
Marlborough
Canterbury
Devizes
Sandwich
Wilton
Waverley
Dover
Salisbury
Winchester
Rye
Romney
Hastings
Winchelsea
Beaulieu
Buckfastleigh

0 25 50 mile
0 25 50 km

56°
54°
52°
50°

A B 2° C 0° D 2°

50 THE FRIARS, FROM 1221

North Sea

Irish Sea

English Channel

Elgin
Banff
Inverness
Kingussie
Aberdeen
Inverbervie
Montrose
Perth
Dundee
St. Andrews
St. Monan's
Cupar
Stirling
Aberdour
Inverkeithing
Luffness
Linlithgow
Haddington
Glasgow
Edinburgh
Irvine
Queensferry
Berwick-upon-Tweed
Lanark
Bamburgh
Roxburgh
Ayr
Hulne
Dumfries
Holystone
Newcastle-upon-Tyne
Wigtown
Carlisle
Kirkcudbright
Penrith
Hartlepool
Appleby
Yarm
Kildale
Northallerton
Stalby
Richmond
Scarborough
Becmachen
Lancaster
York
Beverley
Preston
Kingston-upon-Hull
Pontefract
Doncaster
Grimsby
Warrington
Tickhill
Llanfaes
Rhuddlan
Lincoln
Bangor
Chester
Boston
Burnham Norton
Blakeney
Denbigh
Nottingham
Walsingham
Newcastle under Lyme
Derby
Grantham
Norwich
Stafford
Whaplode
King's Lynn
Yarmouth
Shrewsbury
Lichfield
Leicester
Flixton Gorleston
Brewood
Atherstone
Stamford
Crabhouse
Thetford
Dunwich
Bridgnorth
Coventry
Rothwell
Denney
Bruisyard
Woodhouse
Warwick
Huntingdon
Campsey Ash
Ludlow
Droitwich
Harrold
Orford
Limebrook
Northampton
Bedford
Cambridge
Sudbury
Bury St. Edmunds
Hereford
Worcester
Hitchin
Colchester
Ipswich
Aconbury
Dunstable
Brecon
Aylesbury
Ware
Maldon
Oxford
Kings
Chelmsford
Haverfordwest
Gloucester
Langley
Westminster
London
Carmarthen
Goring
Burnham
Dartford
Minster
Newport
Marlborough
Reading
Sheen
Canterbury
Cardiff
Donnington
Aylesford
Sandwich
Bristol
Lacock
Guildford
Lossenham
Sittingbourne
Buckland
Bridgwater
Ilchester
Sele
Rye
Canonsleigh
Arundel
Lewes
New Romney
Exeter
Chichester
Winchelsea
Bodmin
Cornworthy
Dorchester
Bridport
Plymouth
Dartmouth
Truro

Men:
Austin Friars
Carmelites
Dominican
Franciscan
Crutched
Others
Diocesan boundaries

Women:

0   50   100 miles

0   50   100   150 km

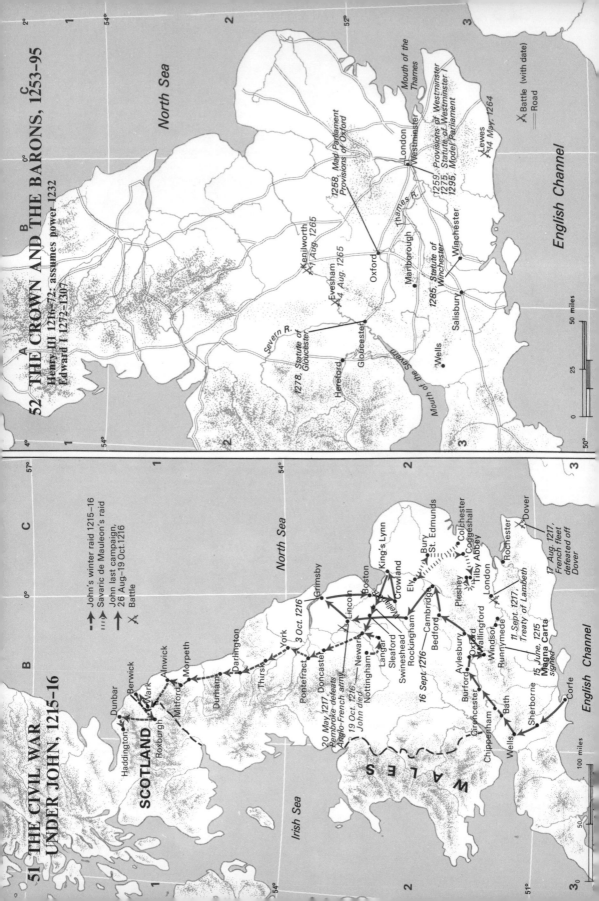

51 THE CIVIL WAR UNDER JOHN, 1215–16

52 THE CROWN AND THE BARONS, 1253–95

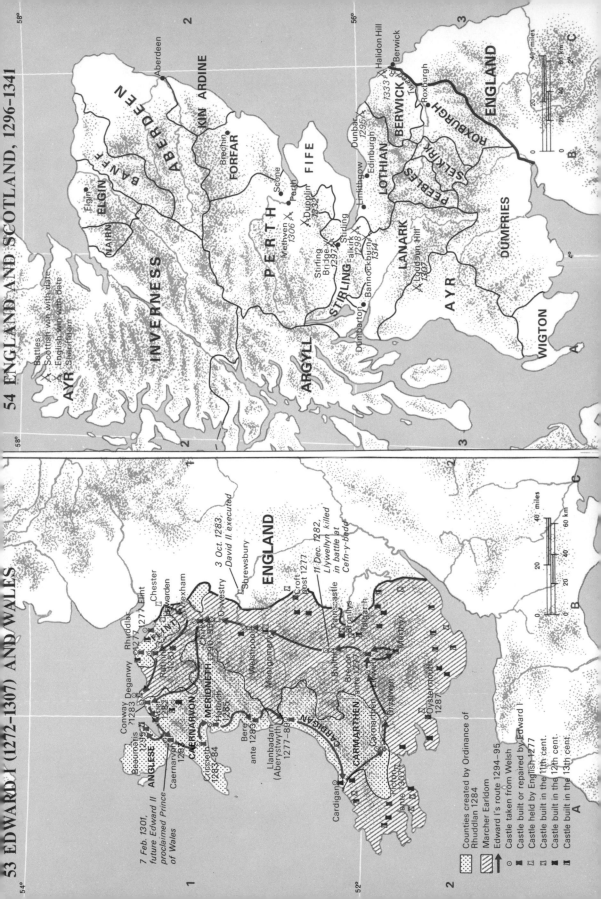

53 EDWARD I (1272–1307) AND WALES

Rhuddlan 1277 1277 Flint
Conway 71283 Deganwy
Chester
Beaumaris 1295 Conway 1283
ANGLESEY
Caernarvon 1283
7 Feb 1301, future Edward II proclaimed Prince of Wales
CAERNARVON
Criccieth 1283–84
Harlech 1285
MERIONETH 1290
Bere ante 1283
Llanbadarn (Aberystwyth) 1277–89
CARDIGAN
Cardigan ante 1300
Kidwelly
Carmarthen
CARMARTHEN
Oystermouth 1287
Ruthin 1281
Dinas Brân
Overton 1279
Wrexham
Whittington 1281
Oswestry
Welshpool
Montgomery
Clun
Builth 1277
Painscastle post 1277
Croft post 1277
Shrewsbury
3 Oct. 1283, David II executed
11 Dec. 1282, Llywelyn killed in battle at Cefn-y-bedd
ENGLAND
Brecon 1277
Radnor
Abergavenny
Wigmore
Newport

Counties created by Ordinance of Rhuddlan 1284
Marcher Earldom
Edward I's route 1294–95
⊙ Castle taken from Welsh
▣ Castle built or repaired by Edward I
▨ Castle held by English 1277
▤ Castle built in the 11th cent.
■ Castle built in the 12th cent.
▣ Castle built in the 13th cent.

0   20   40   60 km
0   20   40 miles

54° 52° 2 1 A B C

54 ENGLAND AND SCOTLAND, 1296–1341

Aberdeen
KINCARDINE
ABERDEEN
BANFF
ELGIN
NAIRN
Elgin
Brechin
FORFAR
INVERNESS
ARGYLL
Scone
Perth
PERTH
Methven 1306
X Dupplin 1332
FIFE
Stirling Bridge 1297
Stirling
Falkirk 1298
Bannockburn 1314
X Loudoun Hill 1307
Dumbarton
STIRLING
LANARK
AYR
WIGTON
DUMFRIES
Dunbar 1296
Linlithgow
Edinburgh
LOTHIAN
PEEBLES
SELKIRK
Halidon Hill 1333
Berwick
BERWICK
Roxburgh
ROXBURGH
Tweed
ENGLAND

Battles
X Scottish win with date
X English win with date
Slewfleam?

0   20   40   60 km
0   20   40 miles

58° 56° 58° 2 3 A B C

North Sea

Irish Sea

Clyde R.

Southern Uplands

Tweed R.

Cheviot Hills

Nith R.

Esk R.

Newcastle

Carlisle

Tyne R.

Hartlepool

Tees R.

Guisborough

Swale R.

Richmond

Scarborough

Ure R.

Ribble R.

Ripon

Bridlington

Lancaster

Wharfe R.

Beverley

Halifax

Aire R.

York

Hull

Ouse R.

Derwent R.

Doncaster

Mersey R.

Lincoln

Bangor

Weaver R.

Derwent R.

Idle R.

Caernarvon

Chester

Dee R.

Derby

Boston

Cambrian Mountains

Stafford

Dove R.

Trent R.

Spalding

Shrewsbury

Lichfield

Grantham

Stamford

Lynn

Norwich

Yare R.

Severn R.

Leicester

Welland R.

Wye R.

B

orth

Coventry

Huntingdon

Waveney R.

Cardigan

Teifi R.

Hereford

Worcester

Daventry

Northampton

Cambridge

Bury St. Edmunds

St. Davids

Avon R.

Ouse R.

Sudbury

Ipswich

Haverfordwest

Brecon

Gloucester

Northleach

Hadleigh

Colchester

Coggeshall

Oxford

Ware

St. Albans

Chiltern Hills

Bristol

Avon R.

Lea

Reading

London

Kenhet

Thames R.

Sandwich

Bridgwater

Exmoor

Mendip Hills

Wey

Guildford

North

Downs

Canterbury

Salisbury

Winchester

Hythe

Dover

Shaftesbury

Avon R.

Test R.

Southampton

Arun R.

Medway

The Weald

Romney

Rye

Chichester

Lewes

Winchelsea

Exeter

Exe R.

Stour R.

Hastings

Tamar R.

Dartmoor

English Channel

0   25   50 miles

0   25   50 km

A   B   C   D

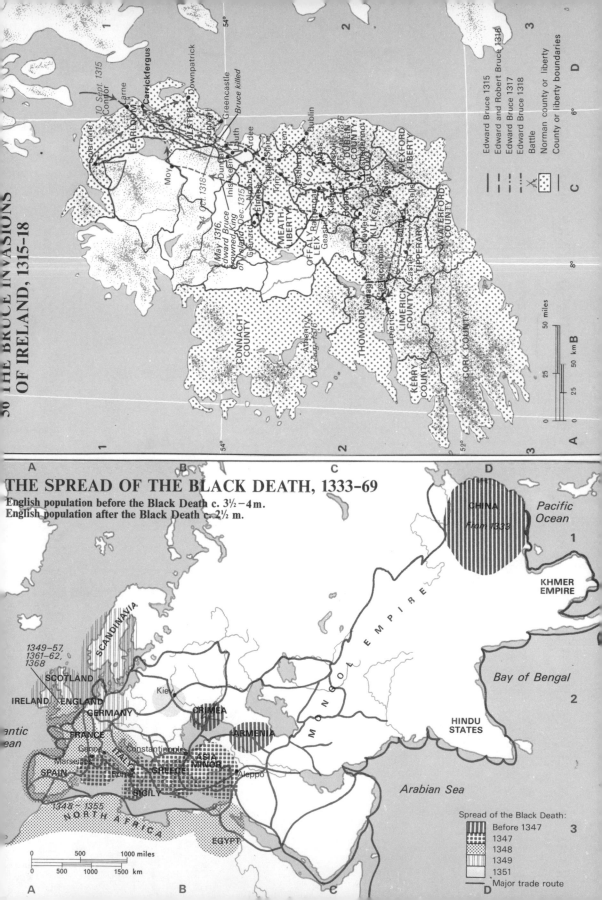

THE SPREAD OF THE BLACK DEATH, 1333–69

30 THE BRUCE INVASIONS OF IRELAND, 1315–18

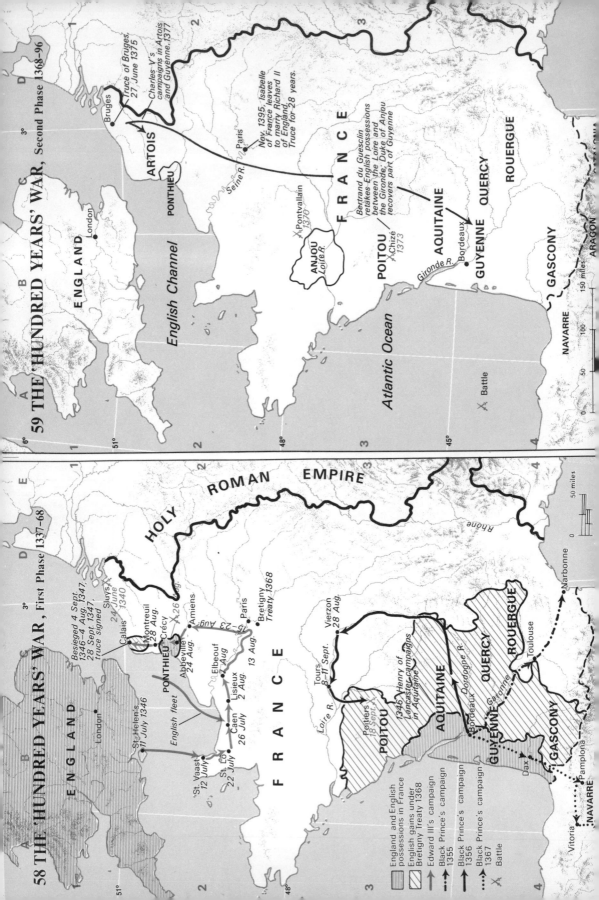

59 THE 'HUNDRED YEARS' WAR, Second Phase 1368–96

58 THE 'HUNDRED YEARS' WAR, First Phase 1337–68

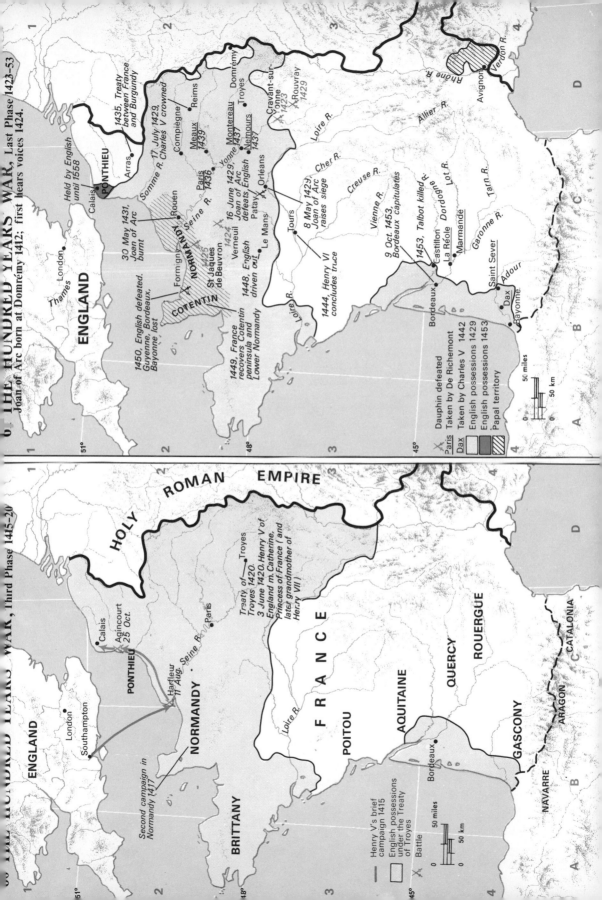

61 THE HUNDRED YEARS' WAR, Last Phase/1423-53. Joan of Arc born at Domrémy 1412; first hears voices 1424.

ENGLAND

Held by English until 1558

1435, Treaty between France and Burgundy

17 July 1429, Charles V crowned

30 May 1431, Joan of Arc burnt

1450, English defeated. Guyenne, Bordeaux, Bayonne lost

1449, France recovers Cotentin peninsula and Lower Normandy

1448, English driven out

1424, English defeat French

16 June 1429, Joan of Arc defeats English

8 May 1429, Joan of Arc raises siege

1444, Henry VI concludes truce

9 Oct. 1453, Bordeaux capitulates

1453, Talbot killed

London · Thames · Calais · PONTHIEU · Arras · Somme R. · Compiègne · Reims · Domrémy · Troyes · Cravant-sur-Yonne 1423 · Rouvray 1429 · Meaux 1439 · Paris 1436 · Rouen · Seine R. · NORMANDY · Formigny · St Jacques de Beuvron 1425 · COTENTIN · Le Mans · Verneuil · Patay · Orleans · Yonne R. · Monterau 1437 · Nemours 1437 · Loire R. · Cher R. · Creuse R. · Loire R. · Tours · Vienne R. · Allier R. · Dordogne R. · Lot R. · Tarn R. · Garonne R. · Castillon · La Réole · Marmande · Saint Sever · Bordeaux · Dax · Bayonne · Adour · Avignon · Rhône R. · Verdon R.

Legend:
- X Paris — Battle
- Dax — Dauphin defeated
- Taken by De Richemont
- Taken by Charles V 1442
- English possessions 1429
- English possessions 1453
- Papal territory

0   50 miles
0   50 km

---

60 THE HUNDRED YEARS' WAR, Third Phase 1415-20.

HOLY ROMAN EMPIRE

ENGLAND · London · Southampton · Calais · Agincourt 25 Oct. · PONTHIEU · Harfleur 11 Aug. 1415 · Seine R. · Paris · Troyes

Treaty of Troyes 1420. 3 June 1420, Henry V of England m. Catherine, Princess of France (and later grandmother of Henry VII)

Second campaign in Normandy 1417

NORMANDY · BRITTANY · Loire R. · F R A N C E · POITOU · AQUITAINE · QUERCY · ROUERGUE · GASCONY · Bordeaux · NAVARRE · ARAGON · CATALONIA

Legend:
- Henry V's brief campaign 1415
- English possessions under the Treaty of Troyes
- X Battle

0   50 miles
0   50 km

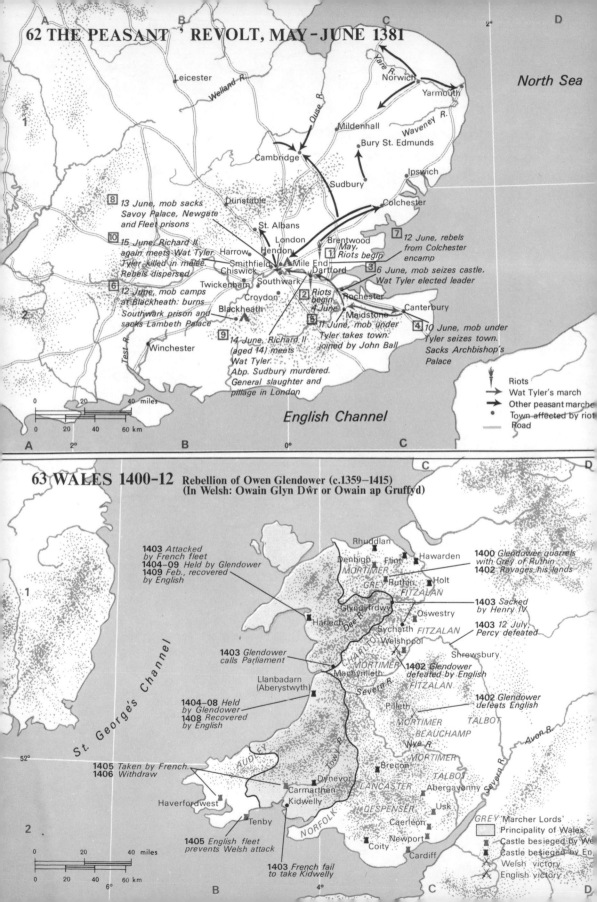

64 ECONOMIC AND SOCIAL LIFE 1400–1500

C   0°   **D**

1

Legend:

- ☺ Port
- ● Principal inland town
- 🎓 University
- Ⓒ Coal
- ⊠ Glass
- △ Iron
- ✦ Wool
- 🐗 Hides
- ▨ Tin
- ⯊ Lead
- 🐏 Cloth

56°

North Sea

2

Aberdeen

St. Andrews

Glasgow   Leith
Clyde R.

Tay R.

Southern Uplands
Tweed R.
Nith R.
Cheviot Hills
Esk R.

Newcastle
Carlisle   Tyne R.
Durham

Pennines

54°

Tees R.
Swale R.
Ure R.
Ouse R.   *Derwent R.*
Wharfe   York
Hull
Ribble R.   *Aire R.*

ISLE OF MAN

Irish Sea

gheda

blin

Liverpool
Mersey R.

Beaumaris
Conway
Caernarvon
Chester
Dee R.

Derwent R.
Idle
Lincoln
Witham R.
Boston

3

Cambrian Mountains
Severn R.
Don R.   Rugeley
Nottingham
Trent R.

Lynn
Yare R.
Norwich
Yarmouth
Waveney R.

Stourbridge
Avon R.
Northampton
Cambridge
Ouse R.
Welland R.
Ipswich

52°

Towy R.   *Wye R.*
Tewkesbury
East Anglian Heights

Haverfordwest
Milford Haven
Tenby
Carmarthen
Chepstow
Gloucester
Woodstock
Oxford
Cotswold Hills
Thames R.
Chiltern Hills
Lea R.

London
Rochester
Medway R.
Sandwich

Bristol
Avon R.
Mendip Hills
Winchester
Test R.
Wey R.
Chiddingfold
The Weald
Romney
Shoreham
Winchelsea

Exmoor
Bridgwater
Exe R.
Parrett R.
Southampton
Arun R.
Pevensey

4

Lyme Regis
Bridport
Stour R.
Poole
Portsmouth
St. Helen's

Tamar R.
Dartmoor
Exeter
Teignmouth
Sidmouth
Otterton
Exmouth
Melcombe Regis
Weymouth
Wareham

Plymouth
Kingswear
Dartmouth

Fowey

St. Ives

English Channel

0   25   50 miles
0   25   50 km

A   4°   **B**   2°   **C**   0°   **D**

65 THE WARS OF THE ROSES, 1455–71, 1485

North Sea

Irish Sea

Legend:
- Lancastrian castle
- Yorkist castle
- Lancastrian victory
- Yorkist victory

Norham
Wark
Bamburgh
Dunstanburgh
25 Apr. 1464
Hedgeley Moor
Alnwick
Warkworth
Hexham
8 May 1468
Newcastle
Lumley
Carlisle
Brancepeth
Raby
Appleby
Skelton
Barnard Castle
Richmond
Bolton
Middleham
Masham
Sheriff Hutton
Lancaster
Knaresborough
York
Spofforth
Cawood
Wressell
Ravenspur 1471
29 March 1461
Towton Moor
Pontefract
30 Dec. 1460
Wakefield
Sandal
Liverpool
Conisborough
Tickhill
Henry VII defeats
Lambert Simnel's rebellion
Rhuddlan
Bolingbroke
Beaumaris
Conway
Chester
Tattershall
Denbigh
Ruthin
Stokefield
16 June 1487
Newark
Harlech
Newcastle-under-Lyme
Belvoir
Tutbury
Castle Rising
Caiste
23 Sept. 1459
Blore Heath
Bosworth Field
22 Aug. 1485
Wingfield
Stokesay
Ludlow
Fotheringhay
Kenilworth
Northampton
10 July 1460
Framlingham
Ludford Bridge
Warwick
1468
Edward IV restored 1471–83
2 Feb. 1461
Mortimer's Cross
Tewkesbury
4 May 1471
Edgcott
1469
Pleshey
St. David's
Grosmont
Skenfrith
Gloucester
St. Albans
22 May 1455
Milford Haven
Haverfordwest
White Castle
17 Feb. 1461
Barnet
14 Apr. 1471
London
Kidwelly
Abergavenny
Raglan
Berkeley
Wallingford
Pembroke
Manorbier
Swansea
Usk
Windsor
Leeds
Caerphilly
Caerphilly
Reigate
Dover
Ogmore
Cardiff
Farnham
Tiverton
Arundel
Steyning
Herstmonceux
Okehampton
Bramber
Pevensey
Portchester
Corfe
Carisbrooke
Compton

English Channel

0   25   50 miles

0   25   50 km

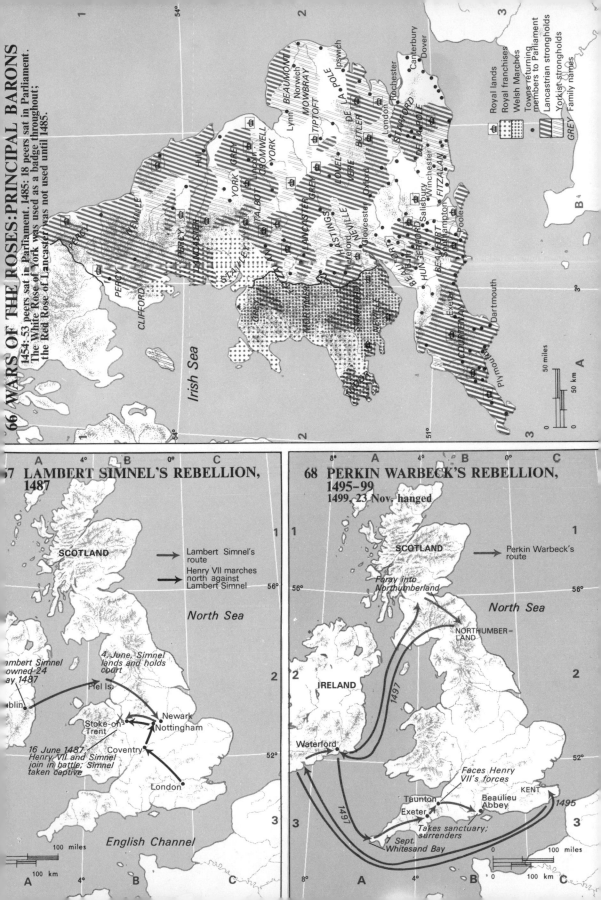

66 WARS OF THE ROSES: PRINCIPAL BARONS

1454–53 peers sat in Parliament. 1485: 18 peers sat in Parliament. The White Rose of York was used as a badge throughout; the Red Rose of Lancaster was not used until 1485.

Legend:
- Royal lands
- Royal franchises
- Welsh Marches
- Towns returning members to Parliament
- Lancastrian strongholds
- Yorkist strongholds
- *GREY* Family names

67 LAMBERT SIMNEL'S REBELLION, 1487

→ Lambert Simnel's route
➡ Henry VII marches north against Lambert Simnel

Lambert Simnel crowned 24 May 1487

4 June, Simnel lands and holds court

16 June 1487 Henry VII and Simnel join in battle; Simnel taken captive

68 PERKIN WARBECK'S REBELLION, 1495–99
1499, 23 Nov. hanged

→ Perkin Warbeck's route

Foray into Northumberland

Faces Henry VII's forces

Takes sanctuary; surrenders

Sept. Whitesand Bay

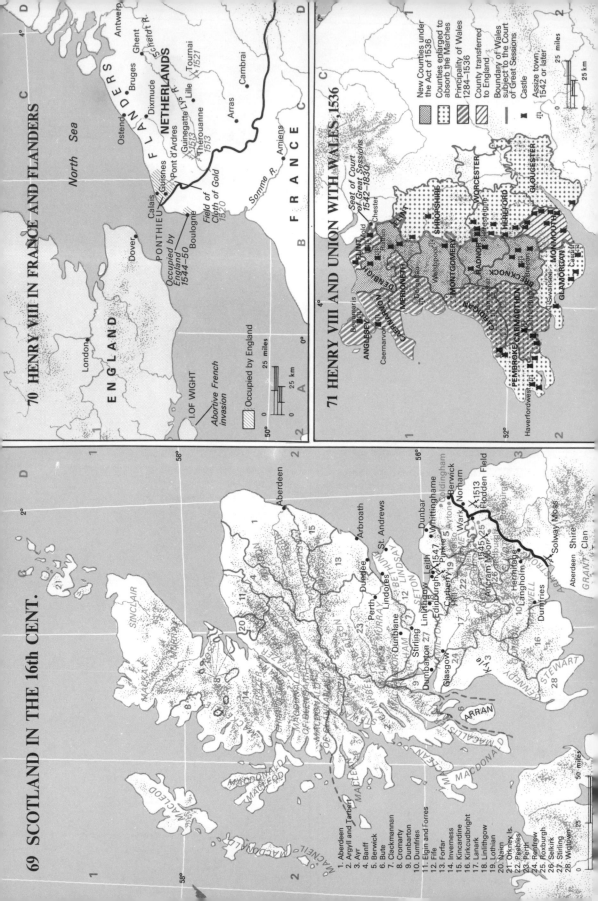

69 SCOTLAND IN THE 16th CENT.

1. Aberdeen
2. Argyll and Tarbert
3. Ayr
4. Banff
5. Berwick
6. Bute
7. Clackmannan
8. Cromarty
9. Dunbarton
10. Dumfries
11. Elgin and Forres
12. Fife
13. Forfar
14. Inverness
15. Kincardine
16. Kirkcudbright
17. Lanark
18. Linlithgow
19. Lothian
20. Nairn
21. Orkney Is.
22. Peebles
23. Perth
24. Renfrew
25. Roxburgh
26. Selkirk
27. Stirling
28. Wigtown

North Sea

Aberdeen
Arbroath
St. Andrews
Dundee
Dunbar
Whittingham
Coldingham
Ayton
Berwick
Norham
Wark
X 1513
Flodden Field
Perth
Dunblane
Lindores
Stirling
Linlithgow
Leith
Edinburgh
X 1547 Pinkie
Carberry Hill
X 1545
Melrose
Jedburgh
X 1545 Ancrum Moor
Hermitage
Langholm
Dumfries
X 1542 Solway Moss
Aberdeen Shire Clan
Glasgow
Dumbarton
ARRAN

SINCLAIR
MACKAY
MACKENZIE
MACLEOD
MACDONALD
CAMPBELL
MACLEAN
MACNEIL
MACALLISTER
KENNEDY
STEWART
MAXWELL
GORDON
HUME
SETON
LINDSAY
BETOUN
MURRAY
GRANT

0   25   50 miles

70 HENRY VIII IN FRANCE AND FLANDERS

North Sea

FLANDERS

NETHERLANDS

Antwerp
Ghent
Bruges
Ostend
Dixmude
Scheldt R.
Guinegatte X 1513
Lille
Tournai X 1521
Cambrai
Thérouanne X 1513
Arras
Pont d'Ardres
Calais
Guines
Boulogne
PONTHIEU
Field of Cloth of Gold 1520
Occupied by England 1544-50
Amiens
Somme R.

FRANCE

ENGLAND

London
Dover
I. OF WIGHT

Abortive French invasion

Occupied by England

0   25 miles

0   25 km

71 HENRY VIII AND UNION WITH WALES, 1536

New Counties under the Act of 1536

Counties enlarged to absorb the Marches

Principality of Wales 1284-1536

County transferred to England

Boundary of Wales subject to the Court of Great Sessions

■ Castle

⬥ Assize town, 1542 or later

Seat of Court of Great Sessions 1542-1830

Chester
Mold
Flint
Ruthin
Denbigh
Beaumaris
ANGLESEY
CAERNARVON
Caernarvon
MERIONETH
Dolgellau
Welshpool
MONTGOMERY
SHROPSHIRE
Shrewsbury
WORCESTER
Worcester
RADNOR
HEREFORD
Hereford
Leominster
CARDIGAN
Cardigan
Aberystwyth
BRECKNOCK
Brecon
MONMOUTH
Monmouth
GLOUCESTER
Gloucester
PEMBROKE
Haverfordwest
CARMARTHEN
Carmarthen
GLAMORGAN
Swansea
Cardiff
FLINT
DENBIGH

0   25 miles

0   25 km

52°

4°

0°

72 THE REFORMATION

Dornoch

Fortrose

Elgin

Aberdeen

Brechin

*John Knox preaching
from 1559 at Dundee,
Perth and St. Andrews*

Lismore

Dunkeld

Iona

Perth

Dundee

Dunblane

St. Andrews

Glasgow

To York

Whithorn

Carlisle

Durham

Jervaulx

Fountains

Bridlington

York

Whalley

Pontefract

CHESTER

Doncaster

Louth

Badings

Lincoln

Kirkstead

Lenton

Norwich

Raphoe

Derry

Connor

Dromore

Down

Killala

Clogher

Armagh

Achonry

Kilmore

Mayo

Elphin

Ardagh

Meath

Tuam

Annaghdown

Clonmacnois

Dublin

Clonfert

ora

Kilmacduagh

Kildare

St. Asaph

Bangor

Chester

Lichfield

Peterborough

Coventry

Ely

Killaloe

Cashel

Ossory

Leighlin

Fern3

Worcester

Hereford

Woburn

Colchester

Limerick

Emly

Gloucester

Oxford

Cork

Lismore

Waterford

St. David's

GLOUCESTER

Oxford

WESTMINISTER

London

oss

Cloyne

Llandaff

Bath

Reading

Rochester

BRISTOL

Wells

Salisbury

Winchester

Canterbury

Glastonbury

Exeter

To Bristol

Chichester

PETERBOROUGH

OXFORD

(for 10 years only)

Dioceses created by Henry VIII

Mainly Lutheran affected area

England: supporting Pilgrimage of Grace
Scotland: mainly loyal to Holy See

Old diocesan boundaries

Cathedral town

Monasteries whose abbots
were executed by Henry VIII

50   100 miles

50   100   150 km

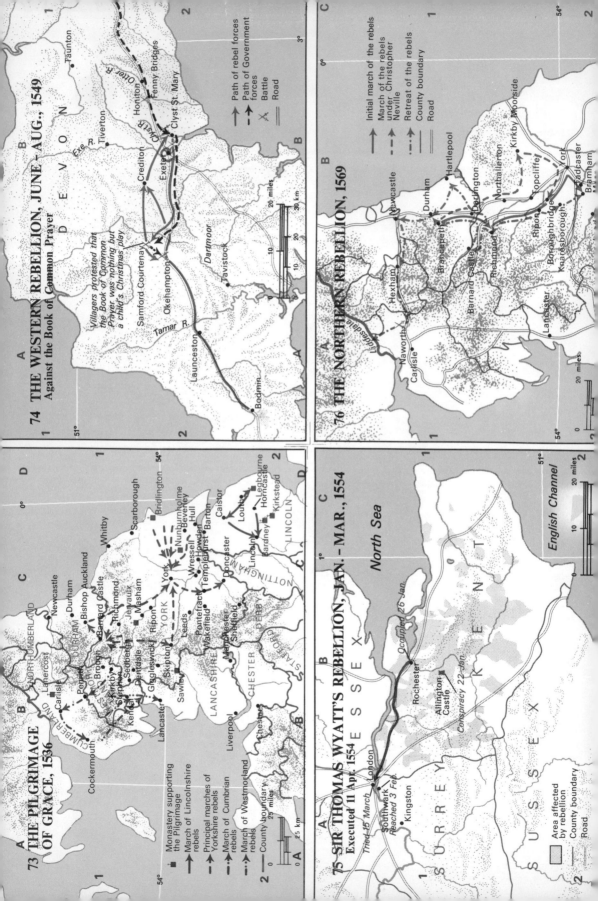

73 THE PILGRIMAGE OF GRACE, 1536

- ■ Monastery supporting the Pilgrimage
- → March of Lincolnshire rebels
- ⇢ Principal marches of Yorkshire rebels
- ⋯⋯ March of Cumbrian rebels
- ⟶ March of Westmorland rebels
- — County boundary

0   25 miles
0   25 km

Taunton · Cockermouth · Carlisle · Lanercost · NORTHUMBERLAND · Newcastle · Durham · Bishop Auckland · Whitby · Scarborough · Bridlington · Penrith · Brough · Barnard Castle · Richmond · Jervaux · CUMBERLAND · Kirkby · Sedbergh · Masham · Kendal · Dentdale · Giggleswick · Ripon · Sawley · York · Nunburnholme · Beverley · Hull · Lancaster · Skipton · Leeds · Wressell · Howden · LANCASHIRE · Liverpool · Pontefract · Wakefield · Templehurst · Barton · Caistor · Louth · Horncastle · Legbourne · Kirkstead · Chester · Manchester · Sheffield · Doncaster · Bardney · LINCOLN · Kington · CHESTER · DERBY · STAFFORD · NOTTINGHAM · YORK · DURHAM

A B C D · 0° · 54° · 1 2

74 THE WESTERN REBELLION, JUNE – AUG., 1549
Against the Book of Common Prayer

- → Path of rebel forces
- ⇠ Path of Government forces
- ✕ Battle
- — Road

Villagers protested that the Book of Common Prayer was 'nothing but a child's Christmas play'

Taunton · Tiverton · Exe R. · Crediton · Honiton · Fenny Bridges · Otter R. · Exeter · Clyst St. Mary · Samford Courtenay · Okehampton · Tavistock · Launceston · Dartmoor · Tamar R. · Bodmin · DEVON

A B · 3° · 51° · 1 2

0   10   20 miles
0   10   20   30 km

75 SIR THOMAS WYATT'S REBELLION, JAN. – MAR., 1554
Executed 11 Apr. 1554

- ▢ Area affected by rebellion
- — Road
- — County boundary

London · Southwark *Reached 3 Feb.* · *Tried 15 March* · Kingston · Rochester · Allington Castle *Conspiracy 22 Jan.* · *Occupied 26 Jan.* · SURREY · SUSSEX · KENT · ESSEX · North Sea · English Channel

A B C · 1° · 51° · 1 2

0   10   20 miles

76 THE NORTHERN REBELLION, 1569

- → Initial march of the rebels
- ⇢ March of the rebels under Christopher Neville
- ⋯⟶ Retreat of the rebels
- — County boundary
- — Road

Newcastle · Hexham · Naworth · Carlisle · Hartlepool · Durham · Brancepeth · Barnard Castle · Darlington · Northallerton · Richmond · Kirkby Moorside · Ripon · Topcliffe · York · Tadcaster · Boroughbridge · Knaresborough · Branham · Lancaster · Ripon · Kidderdale

A B C · 0° · 54° · 1 2

0   20 miles

ENGLAND AND IRELAND, 1553–1640

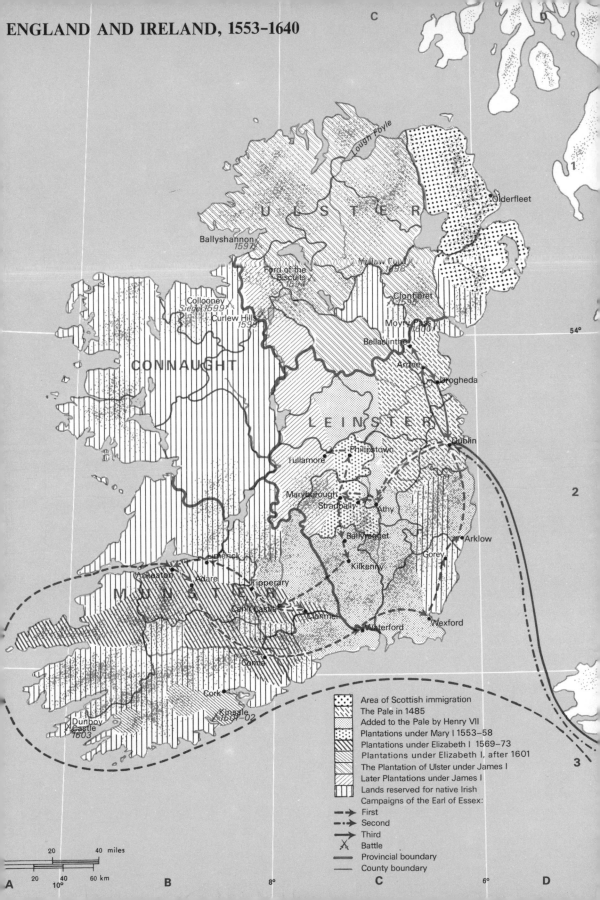

C

D

1

Olderfleet

U L S T E R

Ballyshannon
1597

Ford of the
Biscuits
1594

Mullow Ford
1598

Clontibret
1595

Colloney x
Siege 1599
Curlew Hills
1599

Moyry 1601

54°

Bellaclinthe

CONNAUGHT

Ardee

Drogheda

L E I N S T E R

Dublin

Philipstown

Tullamore

2

Maryborough

Stradbally

Athy

Arklow

Ballyragget

Gorey

Kilkenny

Limerick

Askeaton

Adare

Tipperary

M U N S T E R

Cahir Castle

Clonmel

Waterford

Wexford

Conna

Cork

Kinsale
1601–02

Dunboy
Castle
1603

3

	Area of Scottish immigration
	The Pale in 1485
	Added to the Pale by Henry VII
	Plantations under Mary I 1553–58
	Plantations under Elizabeth I 1569–73
	Plantations under Elizabeth I, after 1601
	The Plantation of Ulster under James I
	Later Plantations under James I
	Lands reserved for native Irish

Campaigns of the Earl of Essex:
- → First
- ⇢ Second
- → Third
- x Battle
- Provincial boundary
- County boundary

20   40 miles

20 40 60 km

10°

A   B   8°   C   6°   D

78 ECONOMIC AND SOCIAL LIFE UNDER THE TUDORS

Population: 1570 – 4.1 m.
 1600 – 4.8 m.

Thames R.	Navigable river
	Lead
	Tin
	Coal
	Iron
	Toolmakers
	Loriners
	Mailers
	Nails
	Salt
	Cloth
	Wool
	Cotton
	Armaments
	Glass
	Dockyards
	Alum
	University
	Chief port
	Road

North Sea

Sea route bringing coal from Newcastle to London

Irish Sea

St. Andrews

Glasgow

Leith

Newcastle

Kendal

Whitby

Malton

Hull

Blackburn

Bury

Rochdale

WEST RIDING

Humber

Liverpool

Beaumaris

Conway

Caernarvon

Chester

DERBY-
SHIRE

Idle

Newark

Boston

Nantwich

Nottingham

Lynn

Oswestry

Stafford

Shrewsbury

Norwich

Yarmouth

Severn R.

Kidderminister

Clee Hills

Birmingham

Droitwich

Cambridge

Ipswich

Worcester

Hereford

Forest
of
Dean

Tewkesbury

Gloucester

Severn Basin

Oxford

Haverfordwest

Milford Haven

Tenby

Chepstow

London

Deptford

Woolwich

Rochester

Chatham

Canterbury

Sandw

Bristol

Mendips

WILTSHIRE

The Weald

Bridgwater

SOMERSET

HAMPSHIRE

Romney

DEVON

Lyme
Regis

Southampton

Shoreham

Winchelsea

Sidmouth

Bridport

Poole

Portsmouth

Pevensey

Exeter

Teignmouth

Otterton

Exmouth

Weymouth

Melcombe
Regis

Wareham

St. Helen's

Plymouth

Kingswear

St. Ives

CORNWALL

Fowey

Dartmouth

English Channel

0	25	50 miles
0	25	50 km

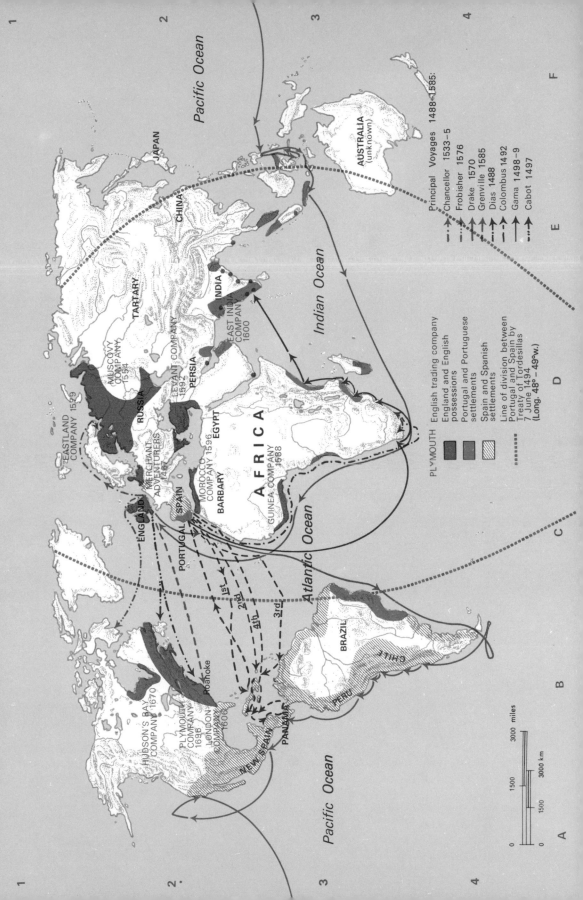

1580-1640: Portugal under the Spanish Crown

Pacific Ocean

JAPAN

CHINA

TARTARY

INDIA

EAST INDIA
COMPANY
1600

Indian Ocean

AUSTRALIA
(unknown)

Principal Voyages 1488–1585:

Chancellor 1533–5
Frobisher 1576
Drake 1570
Grenville 1585
Dias 1488
Colombus 1492
Gama 1498–9
Cabot 1497

MUSCOVY
COMPANY
1554

RUSSIA

PERSIA

LEVANT COMPANY
1592

EASTLAND
COMPANY 1579

EGYPT

MOROCCO
COMPANY 1596

BARBARY

A F R I C A

GUINEA COMPANY
1588

MERCHANT
ADVENTURERS
1465

ENGLAND

PORTUGAL SPAIN

Atlantic Ocean

PLYMOUTH   English trading company
            England and English
            possessions
            Portugal and Portuguese
            settlements
            Spain and Spanish
            settlements
            Line of division between
            Portugal and Spain by
            Treaty of Tordesillas
            7 June 1494
            (Long. 48°–49°w.)

HUDSON'S BAY
COMPANY 1670

PLYMOUTH
COMPANY
1606

LONDON
COMPANY
1606

Roanoke

NEW SPAIN

PANAMA

PERU

BRAZIL

CHILE

1st
2nd
4th
3rd

Pacific Ocean

0   1500   3000 miles
0   1500   3000 km

80 ELIZABETH I AND SPAIN, 1572-96

SCOTLAND

North Sea

23 July 1588: Howard pursues fleeing Armada

1580, 'Jesuit invasion': attempted Spanish invasion foiled

Leicester in the Netherlands 1585-87

Zutphen

UNITED NETHERLANDS

IRELAND

Smerwick

ENGLAND

Amsterdam

The Hague

Utrecht

Nymegen

Flushing

Breda

197 English ships, mostly small; 16,000 to 17,000 men. 100 ships at Plymouth

22 July 1588: Armada attacked by fireships

Bruges

Antwerp

Ypres

Ghent

Maastricht

Gravelines

Brussels

23 July 1588

Calais

SPANISH NETHERLANDS

CORNWALL

Portland

I.O.W.

20 July 1588

Rhine

50°

Plymouth

Lizard

19 July 1588

Atlantic Ocean

14 July 1588

1596, Calais seized by Spain

1591, Azores: Sir Richard Grenville takes on Spanish fleet in the 'Revenge'

FRANCE

2

Armada scattered by squalls

La Coruña

Santander

Finisterre

4 June 1588

Mediterranean Sea

1583, Spanish conquest of England determined

Madrid

40° 1589, English attack on Portugal

Tagus R.

Lisbon

SPAIN

P O R T U G A L

3

Armada leaves with 132 ships and 29,687 men

1587, Drake destroys fleet and stores. 1596, Raided by Earl of Essex and Raleigh

	Spanish territory
→	Route of the Armada 1588
✳	Armada sighted with date

0   100   200 miles

0 100 200 km

Cadiz

A   10°   B   C

THE CIVIL WAR, 1642-53

SCOTLAND

A B C D 2° E 2°

1

56°

Philiphaugh
1645 ✕

NORTHUMBERLAND

Newburn ✕ Newcastle
1640

Durham

2

54°

Marston Moor ✕ York
1644

Preston ✕   Adwalton Moor   Hull
1648   ✕1643

Gainsborough ✕

Rowton Heath ✕   Winceby ✕
1645

Nantwich   1646 May, Charles
✕1644   surrenders to Scots
                              Newark
                    Nottingham

Lichfield   3

                              Naseby ✕
                              1645   Huntingdon
Holmby House ✕   Newmarket
Edge Hill ✕
1642   Cropredy ✕
Worcester ✕   1644

                                    52°

Oxford   EASTERN ASSOCIATION
                    to raise Parliamentary
Lansdown Hill   Army 1643
1643   Uxbridge ✕
Donnington   Windsor   London
Castle   Turnham Green
Roundway Down Newbury Hampton Court
1643 ✕   1644   Basing House
                         ✕1645

Langport ✕
1645
Bideford

Stratton ✕   4

Bradock Down   Hurst Castle Carisbrooke Castle
Lostwithiel ✕✕
1644   Plymouth Dartmouth   IS. OF WIGHT

d for the King
John Grenville
il 1653

LY ISLES

B   4°   C   2°   D   E
                                              0°

Legend:

▨ Area controlled by Parliament at 1 May 1643

░ Area controlled by Parliament at 1 Nov. 1644

✕ Battle

0   25   50 miles
0   25   50 km

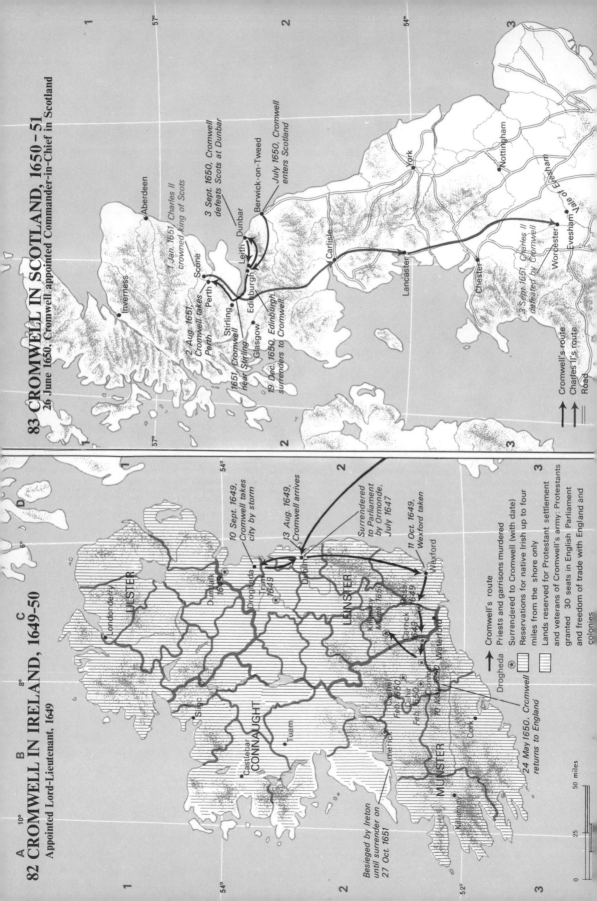

82 CROMWELL IN IRELAND, 1649-50

Appointed Lord-Lieutenant, 1649

ULSTER

Londonderry

Sligo

CONNAUGHT

Castlebar

Tuam

Besieged by Ireton until surrender on 27 Oct. 1651

Limerick

MUNSTER

Killarney

Cork

LEINSTER

10 Sept. 1649, Cromwell takes city by storm

Drogheda

Trim 1649

13 Aug. 1649, Cromwell arrives

Dublin

Surrendered to Parliament by Ormonde, July 1647

11 Oct. 1649, Wexford taken

Wexford

Waterford

24 May 1650. Cromwell returns to England

→ Cromwell's route

⊛ Priests and garrisons murdered

Drogheda Surrendered to Cromwell (with date)

Reservations for native Irish up to four miles from the shore only

Lands reserved for Protestant settlement and veterans of Cromwell's army: Protestants granted 30 seats in English Parliament and freedom of trade with England and colonies

0   25   50 miles

83 CROMWELL IN SCOTLAND, 1650–51

26 June 1650, Cromwell appointed Commander-in-Chief in Scotland

Inverness

Aberdeen

1 Jan. 1651, Charles II crowned king of Scots

Scone

Perth

2 Aug. 1651, Cromwell takes Perth

Stirling

1651 Cromwell near Stirling

Glasgow

Edinburgh

19 Dec. 1650, Edinburgh surrenders to Cromwell

Leith

Dunbar

3 Sept. 1650, Cromwell defeats Scots at Dunbar

Berwick-on-Tweed

July 1650, Cromwell enters Scotland

Carlisle

Lancaster

Chester

York

Nottingham

3 Sept. 1651, Charles II defeated by Cromwell

Worcester

Evesham

Vale of Evesham

→ Cromwell's route

→ Charles II's route

═ Road

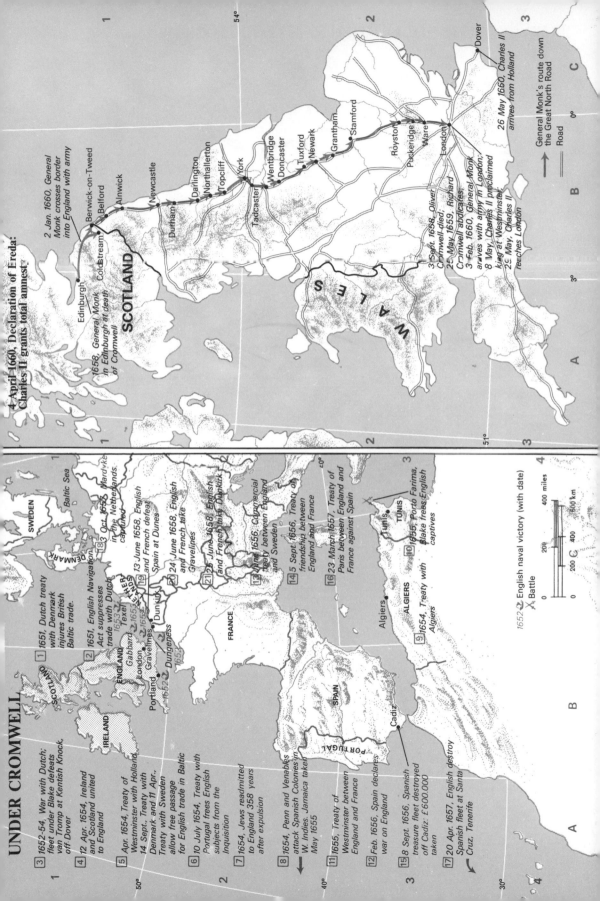

UNDER CROMWELL

4 April 1660, Declaration of Breda: Charles II grants total amnesty

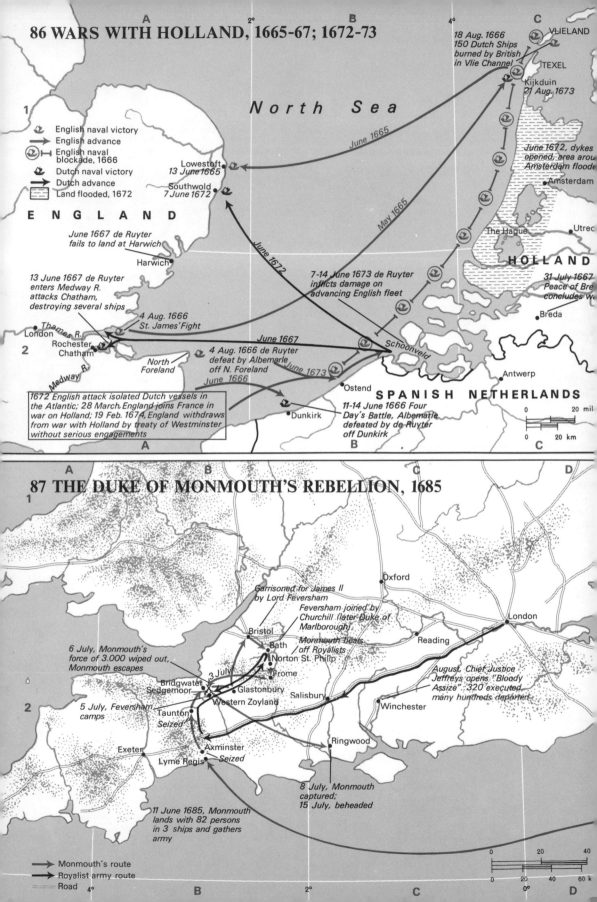

86 WARS WITH HOLLAND, 1665-67; 1672-73

North Sea

18 Aug. 1666
150 Dutch Ships
burned by British
in Vlie Channel

VLIELAND

TEXEL

Kijkduin
21 Aug. 1673

June 1672, dykes
opened, area arou
Amsterdam floode

Amsterdam

English naval victory
English advance
English naval blockade, 1666
Dutch naval victory
Dutch advance
Land flooded, 1672

Lowestoft
13 June 1665

Southwold
7 June 1672

June 1665

May 1665

The Hague

Utrec

H O L L A N D

E N G L A N D

June 1667 de Ruyter
fails to land at Harwich

Harwich

13 June 1667 de Ruyter
enters Medway R.
attacks Chatham,
destroying several ships

4 Aug. 1666
St. James' Fight

7-14 June 1673 de Ruyter
inflicts damage on
advancing English fleet

31 July 1667
Peace of Bre
concludes w

Breda

London
Thames R.
Rochester
Chatham

Medway R.

North
Foreland

4 Aug. 1666 de Ruyter
defeat by Albemarle
off N. Foreland

June 1667

June 1673

June 1666

Schoonveld

Antwerp

1672 English attack isolated Dutch vessels in
the Atlantic; 28 March, England joins France in
war on Holland; 19 Feb. 1674, England withdraws
from war with Holland by treaty of Westminster
without serious engagements

Dunkirk

Ostend

11-14 June 1666 Four
Day's Battle, Albemarle
defeated by de Ruyter
off Dunkirk

S P A N I S H   N E T H E R L A N D S

0   20 mil
0   20 km

87 THE DUKE OF MONMOUTH'S REBELLION, 1685

Oxford

London

Garrisoned for James II
by Lord Feversham

Feversham joined by
Churchill (later Duke of
Marlborough)

Bristol

Bath

Monmouth beats
off Royalists

Norton St. Philip

Reading

6 July, Monmouth's
force of 3,000 wiped out,
Monmouth escapes

3 July

Frome

August, Chief Justice
Jeffreys opens "Bloody
Assize": 320 executed,
many hundreds deported

Bridgwater
Sedgemoor

Glastonbury

Western Zoyland

Salisbury

Winchester

5 July, Feversham
camps

Taunton
Seized

Exeter

Axminster
Seized

Ringwood

Lyme Regis

8 July, Monmouth
captured;
15 July, beheaded

11 June 1685, Monmouth
lands with 82 persons
in 3 ships and gathers
army

Monmouth's route
Royalist army route
Road

0   20   40
0   20   40   60 k

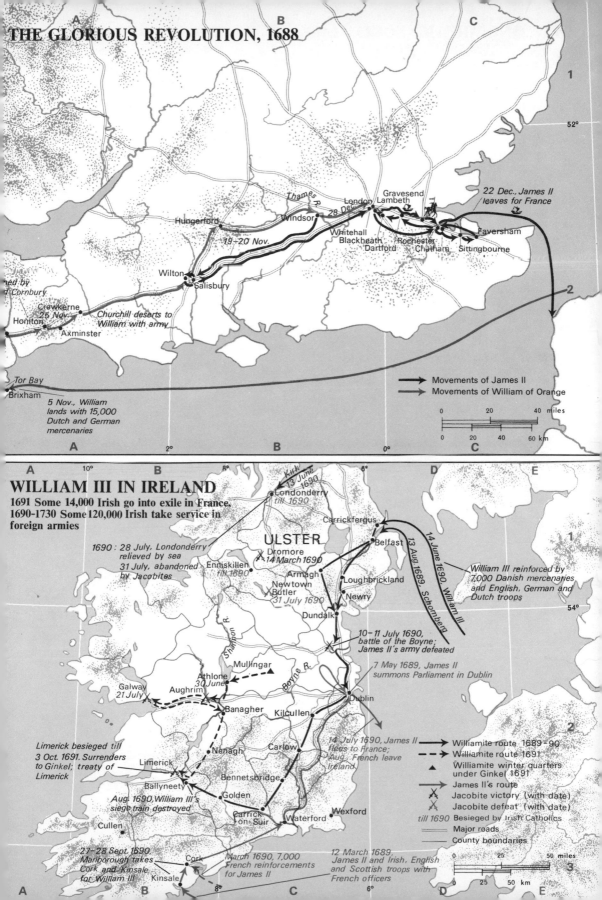

THE GLORIOUS REVOLUTION, 1688

22 Dec., James II leaves for France

Gravesend
Lambeth
London
28 Dec.
Windsor
Thames R.
Whitehall
Blackheath
Dartford
Rochester
Chatham
Sittingbourne
Faversham

Hungerford
19–20 Nov.

...ed by
...d Cornbury

Wilton
Salisbury

Crewkerne
25 Nov.
Honiton
Axminster
Churchill deserts to William with army

Tor Bay
Brixham
5 Nov., William lands with 15,000 Dutch and German mercenaries

→ Movements of James II
→ Movements of William of Orange

0   20   40 miles
0 20 40 60 km

52°

WILLIAM III IN IRELAND

1691 Some 14,000 Irish go into exile in France.
1690–1730 Some 120,000 Irish take service in foreign armies

Kirk
13 June 1690
Londonderry till 1690

Carrickfergus

14 June 1690. William III

13 Aug. 1689. Schomberg

Belfast

1690: 28 July, Londonderry relieved by sea
31 July, abandoned by Jacobites

Enniskillen till 1690

Dromore
14 March 1690

Armagh
Newtown
Butler
31 July 1690

Loughbrickland

Newry

William III reinforced by 7,000 Danish mercenaries and English, German and Dutch troops

ULSTER

Dundalk

10–11 July 1690, battle of the Boyne; James II's army defeated

Shannon R.

Boyne R.

Mullingar

7 May 1689, James II summons Parliament in Dublin

Athlone
30 June

Aughrim

Galway
21 July

Banagher

Kilcullen

Dublin

14 July 1690, James II flees to France; Aug. French leave Ireland

Limerick besieged till 3 Oct. 1691. Surrenders to Ginkel; treaty of Limerick

Nenagh

Carlow

Limerick

Ballyneety

Bennetsbridge

Golden

Aug 1690, William III's siege train destroyed

Carrick-on-Suir

Waterford

Wexford

Cullen

27–28 Sept. 1690, Marlborough takes Cork and Kinsale for William III

Cork

Kinsale

March 1690, 7,000 French reinforcements for James II

12 March 1689, James II and Irish, English and Scottish troops with French officers

→ Williamite route 1689–90
⇢ Williamite route 1691
▲ Williamite winter quarters under Ginkel 1691
→ James II's route
✕ Jacobite victory (with date)
✕ Jacobite defeat (with date)
till 1690 Besieged by Irish Catholics
Major roads
County boundaries

0   25   50 miles
0 25 50 km

54°

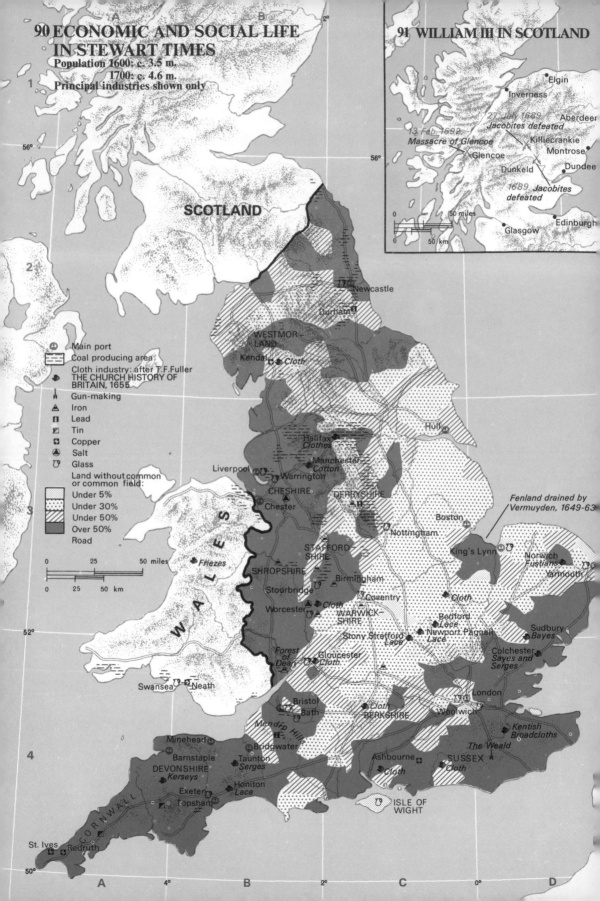

90 ECONOMIC AND SOCIAL LIFE IN STEWART TIMES
Population 1600: c. 3.5 m.
1700: c. 4.6 m.
Principal industries shown only

91 WILLIAM III IN SCOTLAND

SCOTLAND

Main port
Coal producing area
Cloth industry: after T.F.Fuller
THE CHURCH HISTORY OF
BRITAIN, 1655
Gun-making
Iron
Lead
Tin
Copper
Salt
Glass
Land without common
or common field:
Under 5%
Under 30%
Under 50%
Over 50%
Road

0   25   50 miles
0   25   50 km

Inset map (91 William III in Scotland)
Elgin
Inverness
27 July 1689
Jacobites defeated
13 Feb. 1692
Massacre of Glencoe
Aberdeen
Killiecrankie
Glencoe
Montrose
Dunkeld
Dundee
1689 Jacobites
defeated
Glasgow
Edinburgh
56°
0   50 miles
0   50 km

Newcastle
Durham
WESTMOR-
LAND
Kendal
Cloth
Hull
Halifax
Clothes
Manchester
Cotton
Liverpool
Warrington
CHESHIRE
Chester
DERBYSHIRE
Boston
Nottingham
Fenland drained by
Vermuyden, 1649-63
STAFFORD-
SHIRE
King's Lynn
Norwich
Fustians
Yarmouth
SHROPSHIRE
Birmingham
Frezes
Stourbridge
Coventry
Cloth
Worcester
WARWICK-
SHIRE
Bedford
Lace
Sudbury
Bayes
Stony Stretford
Lace
Newport Pagnell
Lace
Colchester
Sayes and
Serges
Forest
of Dean
Gloucester
Cloth
London
Woolwich
Swansea
Neath
Bristol
Bath
BERKSHIRE
Kentish
Broadcloths
Mendip Hills
The Weald
Minehead
Bridgwater
Ashbourne
Cloth
SUSSEX
Cloth
Barnstaple
Taunton
Serges
DEVONSHIRE
Kerseys
Honiton
Lace
Exeter
Topsham
ISLE OF
WIGHT
St. Ives
Redruth
CORNWALL

WALES

56°
52°
50°

WAR OF THE LEAGUE OF AUGSBURG, 1689-1697
(Or the Grand Alliance)

SWEDEN

DENMARK

ENGLAND

Kinsale

Fleurus:
X 1 July 1690,
League defeated

Neerwinden:
X 3 Aug. 1693,
William III
defeated

BRANDENBURG

Steenkirk
X 3 Aug. 1692

SAXONY

Beachy Head
10 July 1690
indecisive

HOLLAND

Ghent

Furnes

Namur:
X 5 June 1692
taken
X 1 Sept. 1695 taken
by William III

28 Dec. 1692 - 7 Jan. 1693
besieged: taken by French

Mons

X 8 Apr. 1691
surrenders

Charleroi

Luxemburg

Mainz

La Hogue

PALATINATE

X 8 Sept. 1689 surrenders

Brest

St. Malo

Paris

Versailles

French repulsed

HOLY
ROMAN
EMPIRE

Atlantic Ocean

FRANCE

SAVOY

VENICE

Stafferda
X 18 Aug. 1690

Marsaglia
X 4 Oct. 1693

Allies as of 9 July 1686
Allies as of 12 May 1689
X French victory with date
X Alliance victory with date

0   100   200 miles
0   100   200 km

PIEDMONT

SPAIN

CATALONIA
X Torroella
27 May 1694

WAR OF THE SPANISH
SUCCESSION, 1702-13

Utrecht

HOLLAND

Venlo
1702

POLAND

SAXONY

Oudenaarde
11 July 1708

Ghent
1708

Kaiserworth
1702

London

Bruges
1708

Bonn
1703

Coblenz

Dunkirk

Brussels

Frankfurt

THE EMPIRE

30 July

SP. NETH.

Malplaquet

Landau

Donauwörth

BAVARIA

Ramillies

Ratisbon

Danube R.

Vienna

Paris

Brabant

Ulm

Blenheim
1704

AUSTRIA

Villmont

Marlborough's route
to Blenheim
Prince Eugene's route
Route of French and
Bavarians under Tallard
Fortress held by Allies
Fortress held by French
Allied victory
French victory
England and her allies
France and her allies
Taken by British

SWITZERLAND

HUNGARY

FRANCE

SAVOY

Torino

Cassano

VENICE

Legnago

Cremona

Luzzara

Patrna

Carpi

Vigo
1702

PORTUGAL

Saragossa

Salamanca

Villa Viciosa
X 10 Dec. 1710
Brihuega
9 Dec. 1710

CATALONIA

Barcelona
1705

SARDINIA

Madrid

Alcantara

Talavera

Almenara
X 27 July 1710

MINORCA
Sept. 1708

Aug. 1708

Lisbon

Alcantara

S P A I N

Valencia

Denia

Almanza
X 25 Apr. 1707

Alicante
1709

SICILY

Cadiz

Gibraltar

0   100   200 miles
0   100   200 km

94 BRITISH POSSESSIONS AFTER THE PEACE OF UTRECHT, 1713
Europe and America

1707, Union between
England and Scotland:
GREAT BRITAIN

Britain granted right
to transport 4,800 slaves
annually to Spanish America

France grants Britain
right to load produce

Atlantic Ocean

Gulf of Benin

Hudson Bay

HUDSON'S BAY COMPANY

NEWFOUNDLAND

MAINE
NEW HAMPSHIRE
NOVA SCOTIA
MASSACHUSETTS
RHODE ISLAND
CONNECTICUT
NEW YORK
NEW JERSEY
PENNSYLVANIA
DELAWARE
MARYLAND
VIRGINIA
NORTH CAROLINA
SOUTH CAROLINA

WEST INDIES

SCOTLAND
IRELAND
ENGLAND

HOLY
ROMAN
EMPIRE
AUSTRIA
HUNGARY
FRANCE
SAVOY
SARDINIA
SICILY
SPAIN
MINORCA
1708
Gibraltar

British possessions
Spanish possessions
French possessions
Austrian possessions
House of Savoy

0   500   1000 miles

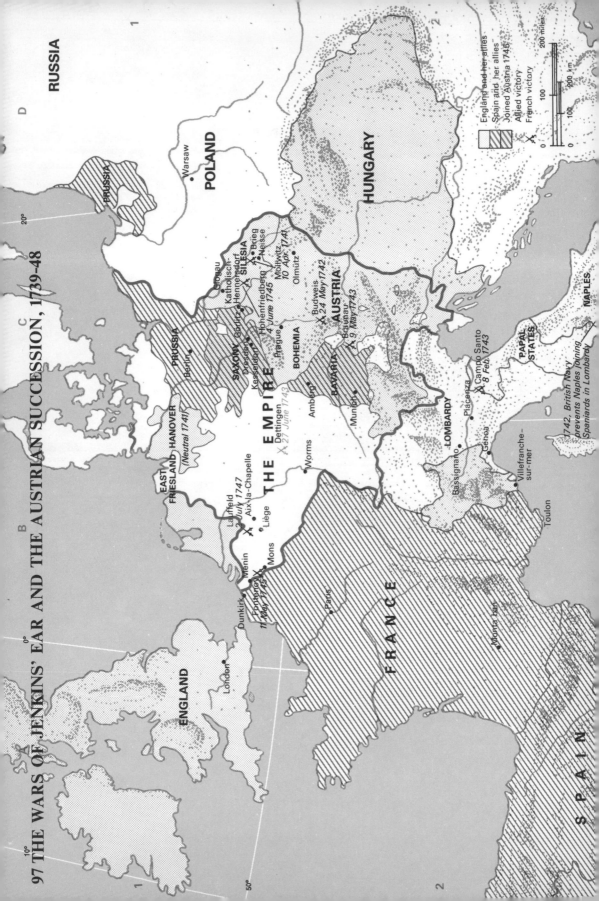

97 THE WARS OF JENKINS' EAR AND THE AUSTRIAN SUCCESSION, 1739-48

RUSSIA

POLAND
• Warsaw

PRUSSIA

Grossau
Katholisch •
Gödic• Hennersdorf
• Brieg
• Neisse
SILESIA
Hohenfriedberg
4 June 1745
Mollwitz
10 Apr. 1741
Olmütz •
Kesselsdorf
Dresden •
Berlin •
SAXONY
PRUSSIA
Budweis
X 24 May 1742
AUSTRIA
HUNGARY
Prague •
BOHEMIA
Braunau
X 9 May 1743

Amberg •
BAVARIA
• Munich

THE EMPIRE

EAST FRIESLAND HANOVER
(Neutral 1741)

Worms •

Dettingen
X 27 June 1743

Aix-la-Chapelle
Lauffeld
2 July 1747
• Liège
• Menin • Mons
Dunkirk •
Fontenoy
11 May 1745

London •
ENGLAND

FRANCE

Paris •

• Montauban

SPAIN

LOMBARDY
Placenza •
X Campo Santo
8 Feb. 1743
• Genoa
Bassignano •
Villefranche-
sur-mer
PAPAL
STATES
NAPLES

Toulon •

1742, British Navy
prevents Naples joining
Spaniards in Lombardy

England and her allies
Spain and her allies
Joined Austria 1745
Allied victory
X French victory

0   100   200 km
0   100   200 miles

98 THE SEVEN YEARS' WAR, 1756-63
(See also maps 99 and 100)

Prussia and her allies (Great Britain and Hanover united from 1714)

Prussia and her allies attack till 1757

Prussia and her allies attack after 1757

Austria and her allies attack till 1757

Austria and her allies attack after 1757

Anglo-Prussian victory

Coalition victory

Boundary of the Holy Roman Empire

DENMARK

HOLSTEIN

Lübeck

Hamburg

Klosterzeven

Stade

Bremen

EAST FRIESLAND

UNITED PROVINCES

HANOVER

Hanover

Brunswick

Magdeburg

Minden 1759

Hastenbeck 26 July 1757

Warburg

Lutterberg

Cassel

Korbach

Bergen 13 April 1759

Mainz

FRANCE

Crefeld 23 June 1758

1757

100 miles

SWEDISH POMERANIA

Rügen

Greifswald

Stralsund

POMERANIA

Kolberg

Stettin

BRANDENBURG

Berlin

Frankfurt

Zorndorf

Kunersdorf 12 Aug. 1759

Küstrin

EAST PRUSSIA

Grossjägersdorf 30 Aug. 1757

Königsberg

Elbing

Danzig

WEST PRUSSIA

Torun

Bromberg

Poznan

Warsaw

POLAND

SILESIA

Liegnitz

Leuthen 5 Dec. 1757

Breslau 22 Oct. 1757

Neisse

Landshut 23 June 1760

Glatz

Moys 7 Sept. 1757

SAXONY

Torgau

Leipzig

Dresden

Freiburg

Lobositz 1 Oct. 1756

Maxen 21 Nov. 1759

Hochkirch 14 Oct. 1758

Zinna

Bautzen

Berkersdorf

Prague

Kolin 18 June 1757

Rossbach

Olmütz

MORAVIA

BOHEMIA

AUSTRIA

BAVARIA

HUNGARY

Krakow

from Russia

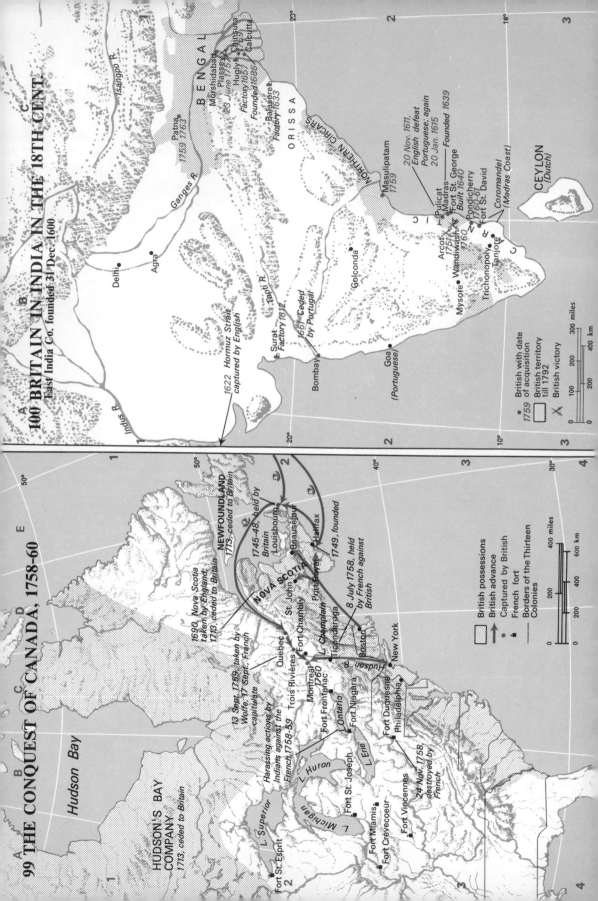

100 BRITAIN IN INDIA, IN THE 18TH CENT.
East India Co. founded 31 Dec. 1600

A   **B**   **C**

Indus R.

Delhi

Agra

Ganges R.

Patna
1759 1763

BENGAL

Murshidabad
Plassey
23 June 1757
Hugly
Factory 1657
Founded 1686

Chinsura
Calcutta

ORISSA

Balasore
Factory 1633

1622 Hormuz Strait captured by English

Surat
Factory 1612

1661 Ceded by Portugal

Bombay

Goa
(Portuguese)

Golconda

Tapti R.

NORTHERN CIRCARS

Masulipatam
1759

20 Nov. 1611, English defeat Portuguese: again 20 Jan. 1615

Pulicat
Madras
Fort St. George
Built 1640
Founded 1639

Arcot
1751
Wandiwash
1760

Mysore

Trichonopoly

Tanjore

Pondicherry
1761-6
Fort St. David

Coromandel (Madras Coast)

CEYLON
(Dutch)

- British with date of acquisition
  1759
- British territory till 1792
- X British victory

0   100   200   300 miles
0   200   400 km

---

99 THE CONQUEST OF CANADA, 1758-60

A   **B**   **C**   **D**   **E**

Hudson Bay

HUDSON'S BAY COMPANY
1713, ceded to Britain

L. Superior

Fort St. Esprit

L. Huron

L. Michigan

Fort St. Joseph

Fort Miamis

Fort Crèvecoeur

Fort Vincennes
24 Nov. 1758, destroyed by French

L. Erie

Fort Niagara

L. Ontario

Fort Frontenac

Fort Duquesne

Philadelphia

Hudson R.

New York

Boston

8 July 1758, held by French against British

Champlain
Ticonderoga

Montreal
1760

Trois Rivières

Fort Chambly

Quebec
13 Sept. 1759, taken by Wolfe, 17 Sept., French capitulate

Harassing actions by Indians against the French, 1758-59

St. John

Port Royal

NOVA SCOTIA
1690, Nova Scotia taken by England, 1713, ceded to Britain

Beauséjour

Halifax
1749, founded

Louisbourg
1745-48, held by Britain

NEWFOUNDLAND
1713, ceded to Britain

- British possessions
- British advance
- French fort
- Borders of the Thirteen Colonies

0   200   400 miles
0   200   400   600 km

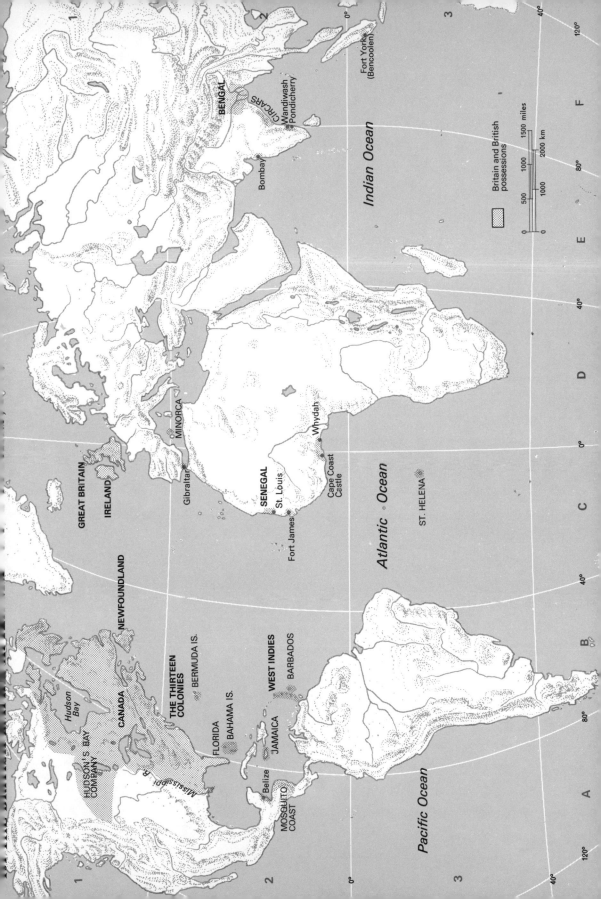

GREAT BRITAIN

IRELAND

NEWFOUNDLAND

CANADA

Hudson Bay

HUDSON'S BAY COMPANY

Mississippi R.

THE THIRTEEN COLONIES

BERMUDA IS.

FLORIDA

BAHAMA IS.

Belize

MOSQUITO COAST

JAMAICA

WEST INDIES

BARBADOS

Pacific Ocean

Atlantic · Ocean

ST. HELENA

Fort James

St. Louis

SENEGAL

Cape Coast Castle

Whydah

Gibraltar

MINORCA

Bombay

BENGAL

CIRCARS

Wandiwash
Pondicherry

Fort York
(Bencoolen)

Indian Ocean

Britain and British
possessions

1500 miles
2000 km
500 1000
1000

0°

40°

80°

120°

0°

40°

80°

120°

A B C D E F

1 2 3

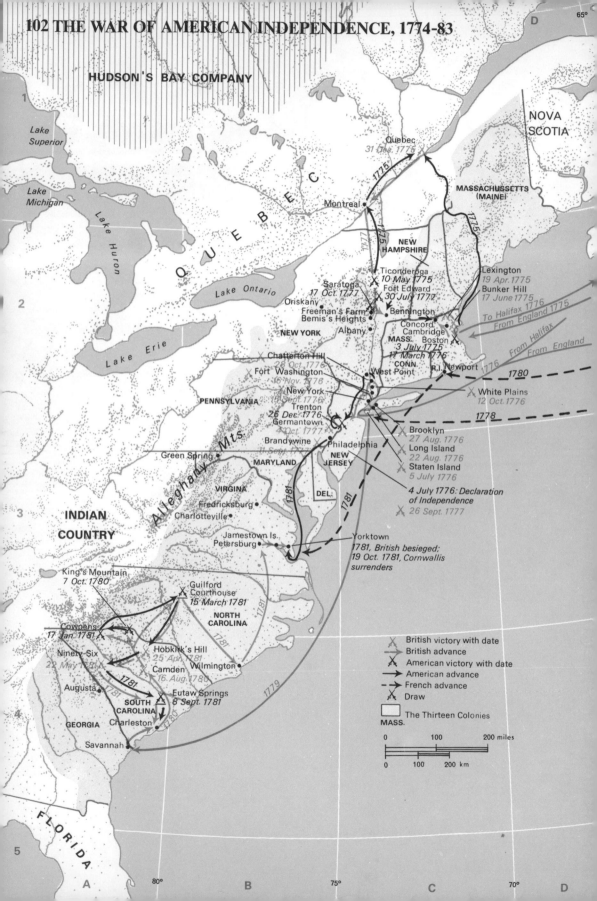

102 THE WAR OF AMERICAN INDEPENDENCE, 1774-83

HUDSON'S BAY COMPANY

NOVA SCOTIA

Lake Superior

Lake Michigan

Lake Huron

Q U E B E C

Lake Ontario

Lake Erie

1775

Quebec
31 Dec. 1775

Montreal

MASSACHUSSETTS (MAINE)

NEW HAMPSHIRE

Ticonderoga
10 May 1775
Fort Edward
30 July 1777

Saratoga
17 Oct. 1777

Oriskany

Freeman's Farm
Bemis's Heights

Bennington

NEW YORK

Albany

Lexington
19 Apr. 1775
Bunker Hill
17 June 1775

Concord
Cambridge
MASS.   Boston
3 July 1775
17 March 1776

To Halifax 1776
From England 1775
From Halifax

Chatterton Hill
28 Oct. 1776

CONN.

West Point

R.I. Newport

1776   From England

Fort Washington
16 Nov. 1776

New York
11 Sept. 1776

PENNSYLVANIA

Trenton
26 Dec. 1776
Germantown
4 Oct. 1777

Brandywine
11 Sept. 1777

Green Spring

Philadelphia

MARYLAND

NEW JERSEY

1780

White Plains
12 Oct. 1776

1778

Brooklyn
27 Aug. 1776
Long Island
22 Aug. 1776
Staten Island
5 July 1776

4 July 1776: Declaration of Independence
26 Sept. 1777

Alleghany Mts.

INDIAN COUNTRY

VIRGINA

Fredricksburg
Charlotteville

Jamestown Is.
Petersburg

DEL.

1781

1781

Yorktown
1781, British besieged; 19 Oct. 1781, Cornwallis surrenders

King's Mountain
7 Oct. 1780

Guilford Courthouse
15 March 1781

NORTH CAROLINA

Cowpens
17 Jan. 1781

Ninety-Six
22 May 1781

Hobkirk's Hill
25 Apr. 1781

Camden
16 Aug. 1780

Wilmington

1781

1781

Augusta

1781

SOUTH CAROLINA

Eutaw Springs
8 Sept. 1781

1779

GEORGIA

Charleston

1781

Savannah

F L O R I D A

British victory with date
British advance
American victory with date
American advance
French advance
Draw

The Thirteen Colonies
MASS.

0   100   200 miles

0   100   200 km

104 PRINCIPAL NAVIGATIONS AND CANALS, 18TH TO 19TH CENTURIES

105 AGRICULTURE IN THE 18TH CENT. (Names of Counties are given on map 122)

105 INDUSTRY AND COMMERCE IN THE 18TH CENT.
(For canals and navigations, see map 104)

Legend:

- **10** Chief town in 1801 with population in thousands
- 'Three cornered' slave trade
- Coal
- Ironworks
- Pottery
- Wool growing area
- Wool manufacturing centre
- Cotton
- Coastal shipping route
- Coach time following improvement of roads
- *1764:* (to London)
- Road

1776: 4 days
Glasgow 77
Edinburgh 82

1776: 3 days
Newcastle 28
Carlisle 10
Sunderland 12
Whitby

1774: 2 days
York 16
Hull 0

Preston
Bradford
Halifax
Leeds 53
Bolton
Wigan 11
Bury
Huddersfield 11
Liverpool 78
Manchester and Salford 84
Stockport 15
Sheffield 31

1781: 2 days
Chester 16
Burslem
Stoke
Lincoln 7

Derby 11
Nottingham 29
Lynn 10
Norwich 37
Yarmouth 15

1764: 2 days
Shrewsbury 15
Broseley
Leicester 17

Coalbrookdale
Bridgnorth
Birmingham 74
Cambridge 10
Ipswich 11

Bewdley
Coventry 16
Colchester 14

Worcester 11

Merthyr Tydfil
Oxford 12

Swansea
Neath

London 900
Reading 10
Southwark 67
Chatham 11

1779: 1-2 days
Bristol 64
Bath 32
Dover 15

Southampton 8
Portsmouth 32

Exeter 17

Plymouth 43

0   25   50 [miles]
0   25   50 km

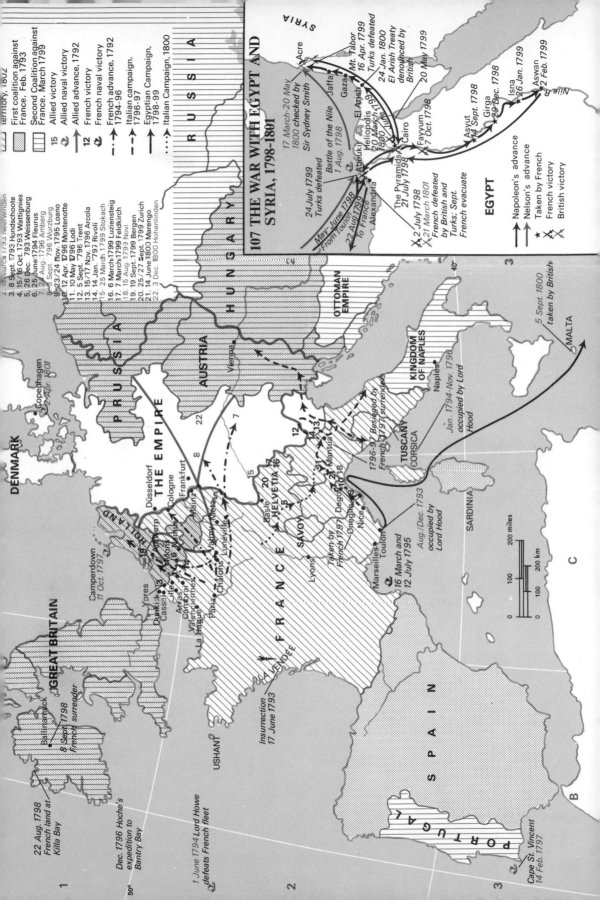

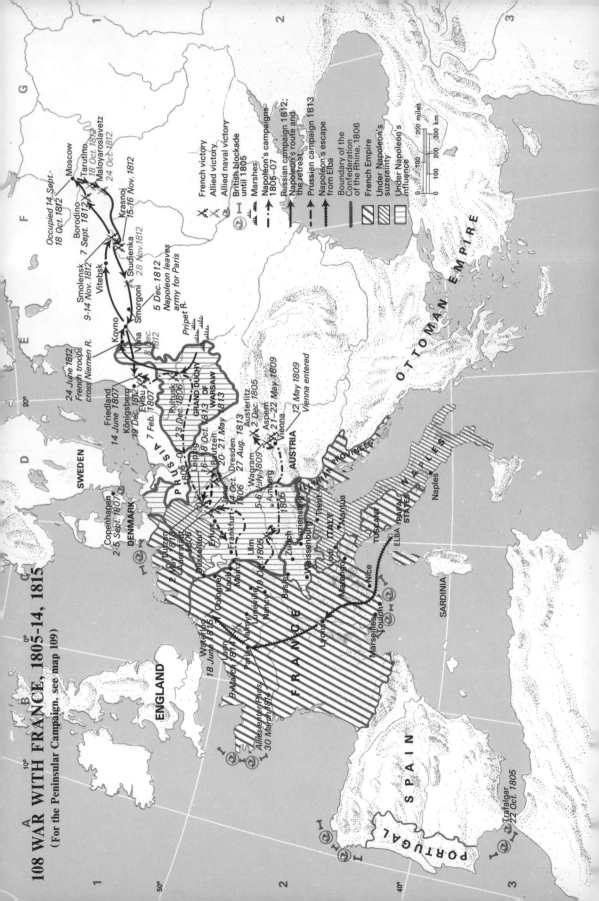

108 WAR WITH FRANCE, 1805–14, 1815

(For the Peninsular Campaign, see map 109)

Legend:

- ✗ French victory
- ✗ Allied victory
- I Allied naval victory
- British blockade until 1805
- Marshes
- Napoleon's campaigns 1805–07
- Russian campaign 1812; Napoleon's route and the retreat
- Prussian campaign 1813
- Napoleon's escape from Elba
- Boundary of the Confederation of the Rhine, 1806
- French Empire
- Under Napoleon's suzerainty
- Under Napoleon's influence

Map labels:

Moscow
Occupied 14 Sept.– 18 Oct. 1812
Tarutino, 18 Oct. 1812
Maloyaroslavets 24 Oct. 1812
Borodino 7 Sept. 1812
Krasnoj 15–16 Nov. 1812
Smolensk 9–14 Nov. 1812
Vitebsk
Studienka 28 Nov. 1812
Smorgoni
5 Dec. 1812 Napoleon leaves army for Paris
Kovno
Vilna 9 Dec. 1812
Pripet R.
24 June 1812 French troops cross Niemen R.
Friedland 14 June 1807
Königsberg 19 Dec. 1812
Eylau 7 Feb. 1807
Pultusk 26 Dec. 1806
GRAND DUCHY OF WARSAW 1813
P R U S S I A
1806–07 23 Dec. 1813
SWEDEN
DENMARK
Copenhagen 2–5 Sept. 1807
Leipzig 16–18 Oct. 1813
Lützen 2 May 1813
Bautzen 20–21 May 1813
Dresden 27 Aug. 1813
Jena 14 Oct. 1806
Auerstädt 1806
Düsseldorf
Erfurt
Cologne
Frankfurt
Mainz
Kaiserslautern
Nancy
Lunéville
Paris
Allies enter Paris 30 March 1814
9 March 1814
Laon
Valmy
Waterloo 18 June 1815
F R A N C E
Lyons
Marseilles
Toulon
Nice
S P A I N
PORTUGAL
Trafalgar 22 Oct. 1805
SARDINIA
ELBA
Napoleon's escape from Elba
TUSCANY
PAPAL STATES
Naples
NAPLES
I T A L Y
Mantua
Marengo
Lodi
Basle
Zurich
Ulm 14 Oct. 1805
Weissenburg
Regensburg
Amberg
Eckmühl
A U S T R I A
Vienna 12 May 1809 Vienna entered
Aspern 21–22 May 1809
Wagram 5–6 July 1809
Austerlitz 2 Dec. 1805
Trent
ILLYRIAN PROVINCES
O T T O M A N   E M P I R E
ENGLAND

Scale: 0 100 200 300 km / 0 100 200 miles

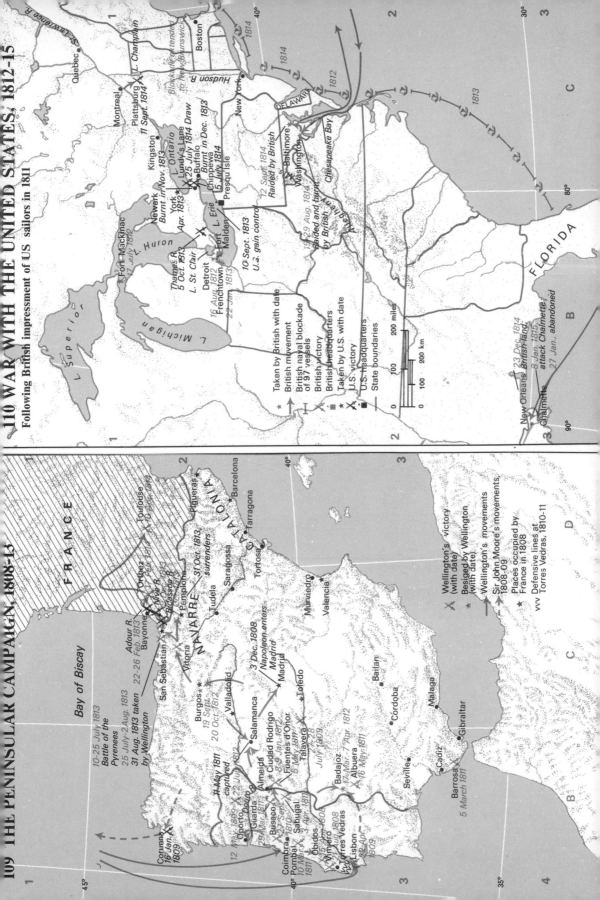

109 THE PENINSULAR CAMPAIGN, 1808-13

110 WAR WITH THE UNITED STATES, 1812-15
Following British impressment of US sailors in 1811

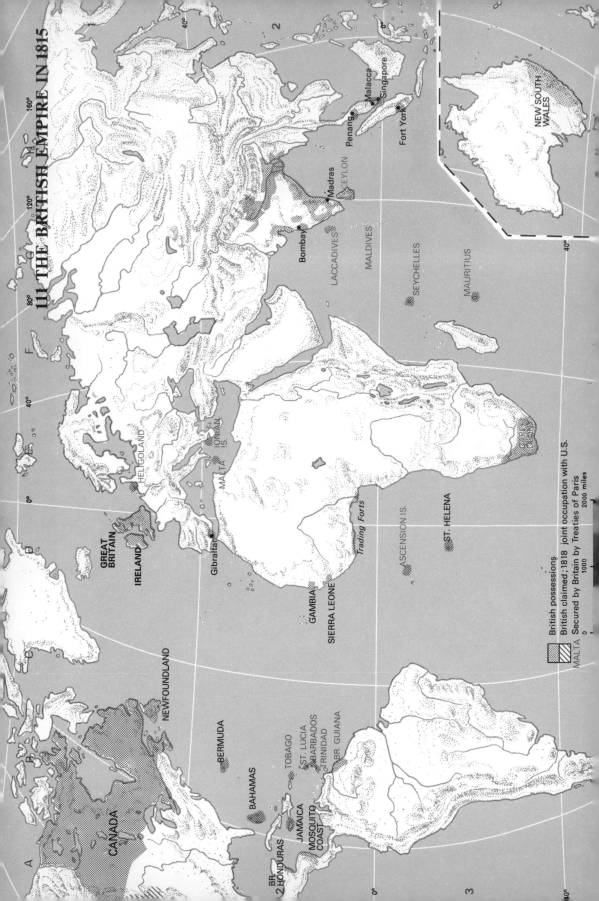

III THE BRITISH EMPIRE IN 1815

NEW SOUTH WALES

Malacca
Singapore
Penang
Fort York
Madras
CEYLON
Bombay
LACCADIVES
MALDIVES
SEYCHELLES
MAURITIUS

HELIGOLAND
MALTA
IONIAN IS.

GREAT BRITAIN
IRELAND
Gibraltar

GAMBIA
SIERRA LEONE
Trading Forts

ASCENSION IS.
ST. HELENA
CAPE COLONY

NEWFOUNDLAND

BERMUDA

TOBAGO
ST. LUCIA
BARBADOS
TRINIDAD
BR. GUIANA

BAHAMAS

JAMAICA
MOSQUITO COAST
BR. HONDURAS

CANADA

British possessions
British claimed;1818 joint occupation with U.S.
Secured by Britain by Treaties of Paris
MALTA

0   1000   2000 miles

112 RAILWAY EXPANSION IN THE 19TH CENT.
It is not possible to show all the branch lines on a map of this scale

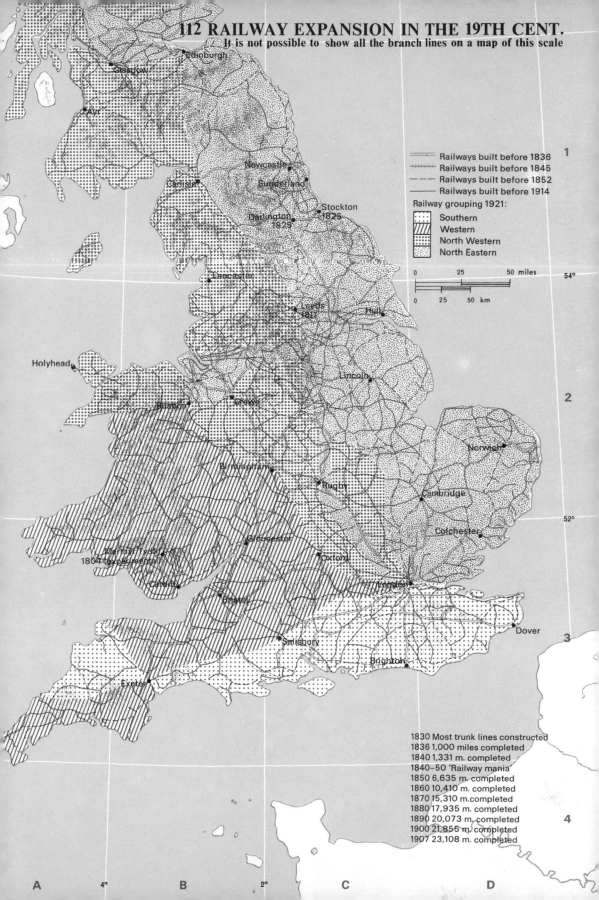

Railways built before 1836
Railways built before 1845
Railways built before 1852
Railways built before 1914

Railway grouping 1921:
Southern
Western
North Western
North Eastern

0   25   50 miles

0   25   50 km

Glasgow

Edinburgh

Ayr

Newcastle

Carlisle

Sunderland

Stockton
1825

Darlington
1825

Lancaster

Leeds
1811

Hull

Holyhead

Ruabon

Crewe

Lincoln

Norwich

Birmingham

Rugby

Cambridge

Gloucester

Colchester

Merthyr Tydfil
1804 experimental

Oxford

London

Cardiff

Bristol

Dover

Salisbury

Brighton

Exeter

1830 Most trunk lines constructed
1836 1,000 miles completed
1840 1,331 m. completed
1840–50 'Railway mania'
1850 6,635 m. completed
1860 10,410 m. completed
1870 15,310 m. completed
1880 17,935 m. completed
1890 20,073 m. completed
1900 21,855 m. completed
1907 23,108 m. completed

54°

52°

1

2

3

4

A   4°   B   2°   C   D

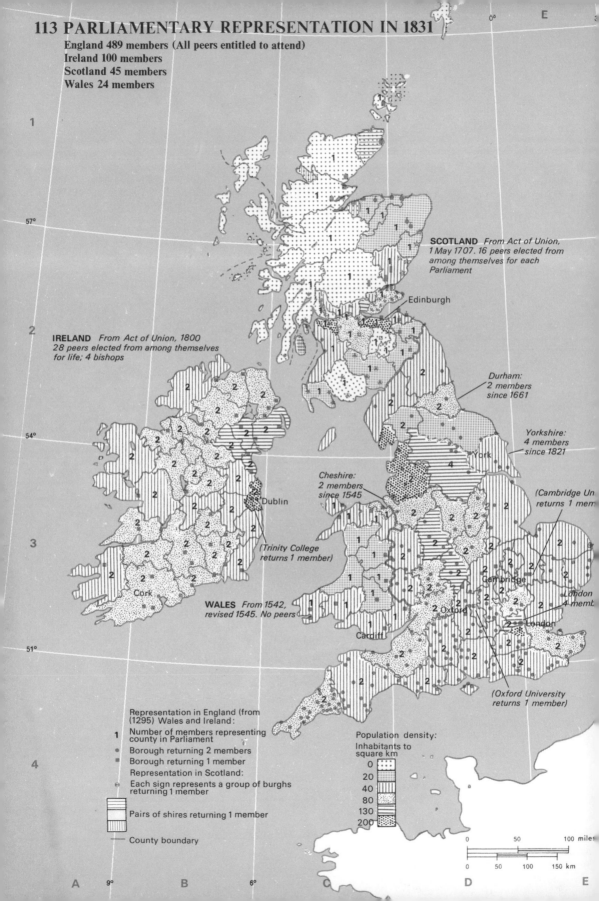

113 PARLIAMENTARY REPRESENTATION IN 1831

England 489 members (All peers entitled to attend)
Ireland 100 members
Scotland 45 members
Wales 24 members

SCOTLAND *From Act of Union,*
1 May 1707. 16 peers elected from
among themselves for each
Parliament

Edinburgh

IRELAND *From Act of Union, 1800*
28 peers elected from among themselves
for life; 4 bishops

Durham:
2 members
since 1661

Yorkshire:
4 members
since 1821

York

Cheshire:
2 members
since 1545

(Cambridge Un.
returns 1 mem

Dublin

(Trinity College
returns 1 member)

Cambridge

London
4 memb

WALES *From 1542,*
revised 1545. No peers

Cork

Oxford

London

Cardiff

(Oxford University
returns 1 member)

Representation in England (from
(1295) Wales and Ireland:

1   Number of members representing
county in Parliament

•   Borough returning 2 members

▪   Borough returning 1 member

Representation in Scotland:

   Each sign represents a group of burghs
returning 1 member

   Pairs of shires returning 1 member

——   County boundary

Population density:
Inhabitants to
square km
0
20
40
80
130
200

0   50   100 miles

0   50   100   150 km

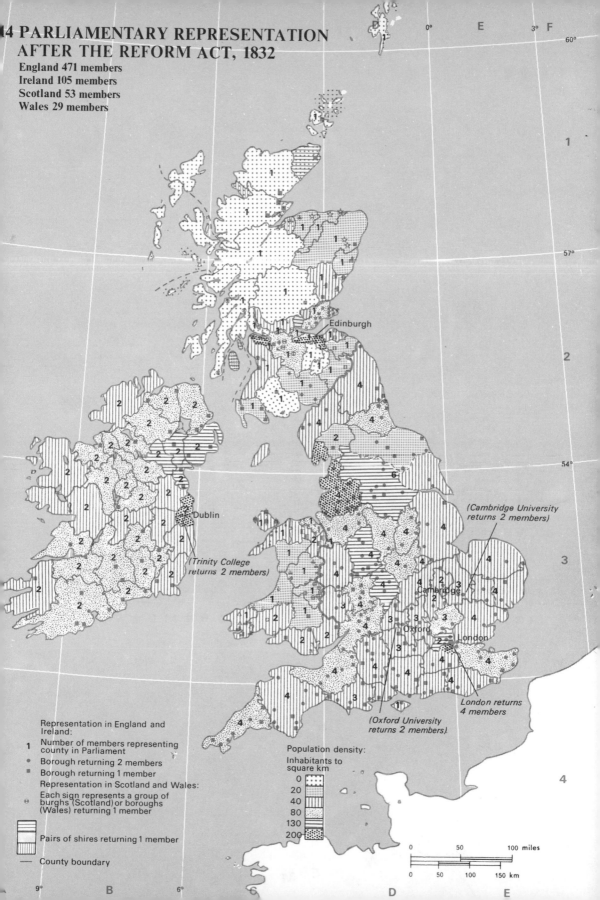

44 PARLIAMENTARY REPRESENTATION
AFTER THE REFORM ACT, 1832

England 471 members
Ireland 105 members
Scotland 53 members
Wales 29 members

Edinburgh

Dublin

(Cambridge University
returns 2 members)

(Trinity College
returns 2 members)

Cambridge

Oxford

London

(Oxford University
returns 2 members)

London returns
4 members

Representation in England and
Ireland:

1 Number of members representing
   county in Parliament

• Borough returning 2 members

▪ Borough returning 1 member

Representation in Scotland and Wales:

Each sign represents a group of
burghs (Scotland) or boroughs
(Wales) returning 1 member

Pairs of shires returning 1 member

— County boundary

Population density:
Inhabitants to
square km

0
20
40
80
130
200

0   50   100 **miles**

0   50   100   150 **km**

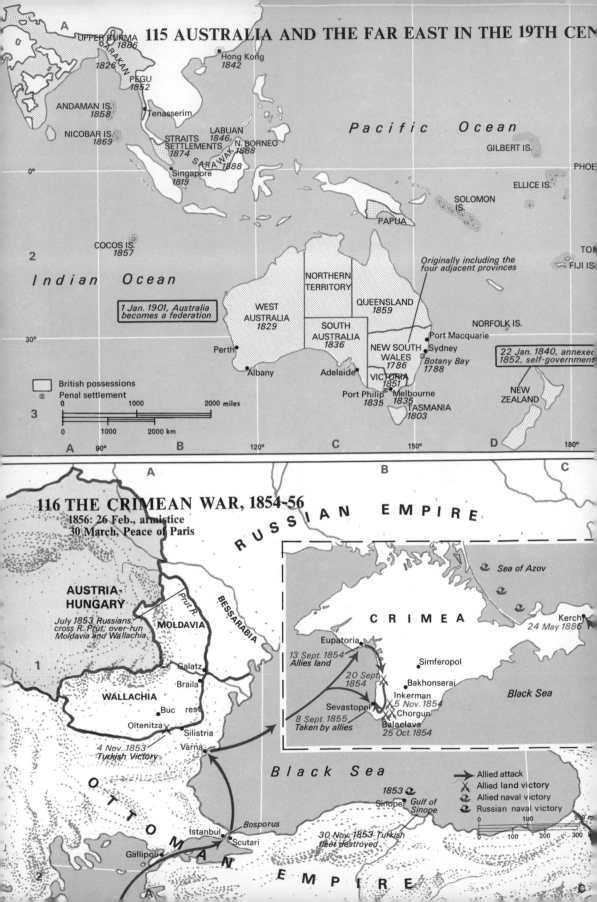

UPPER BURMA
1886
ARAKAN
1826
Hong Kong
1842
PEGU
1852
ANDAMAN IS.
1858
Tenasserim
LABUAN
1846
NICOBAR IS.
1869
STRAITS
SETTLEMENTS
1874
N. BORNEO
1888
SARAWAK *1888*
Singapore
1819

GILBERT IS.

PHOE

Pacific   Ocean

ELLICE IS.

0°

SOLOMON
IS.

PAPUA

Indian   Ocean

COCOS IS.
1857

TO

FIJI IS

2

NORTHERN
TERRITORY

*Originally including the
four adjacent provinces*

WEST
AUSTRALIA
1829

QUEENSLAND
1859

NORFOLK IS.

*1 Jan. 1901, Australia
becomes a federation*

SOUTH
AUSTRALIA
1836

Port Macquarie

30°

Perth

NEW SOUTH
WALES
1786

Sydney

*Botany Bay
1788*

*22 Jan. 1840, annexed
1852, self-government*

Albany

Adelaide

VICTORIA
1851

Port Philip
1835

Melbourne
1835

NEW
ZEALAND

☐ British possessions
▥ Penal settlement

0   1000   2000 miles

TASMANIA
1803

3

0   1000   2000 km

A   90°   B   120°   C   150°   D   180°

116 THE CRIMEAN WAR, 1854-56
1856: 26 Feb., armistice
30 March, Peace of Paris

R U S S I A N   E M P I R E

Sea of Azov

AUSTRIA-
HUNGARY

Prut R.

BESSARABIA

C R I M E A

Kerch
24 May 1885

*July 1853 Russians
cross R. Prut; over-run
Moldavia and Wallachia*

MOLDAVIA

Eupatoria

Simferopol

Galatz

*13 Sept. 1854
Allies land*

*20 Sept.
1854*

Bakhonserai

Black Sea

Braila

WALLACHIA

Buc   rest

Inkerman
5 Nov. 1854

Sevastopol

Chorgun

1

Oltenitza

Silistria

*8 Sept. 1855
Taken by allies*

Balaclava
25 Oct. 1854

*4 Nov. 1853
Turkish Victory*

Varna

Black   Sea

➤ Allied attack
✕ Allied land victory
⚓ Allied naval victory
⚓ Russian naval victory

1853 ⚓

O T T O M A N

Sinope *Gulf of
Sinope*

0   100   200 m

Istanbul

Bosporus

Scutari

*30 Nov. 1853 Turkish
fleet destroyed*

0   100   200   300

Gallipoli

E M P I R E

2

THE AUTONOMY OF CANADA, 1 JULY 1867

	British Dominion
	Annexed to Dominion
	Dominion boundary
	Canadian Pacific Railway completed 7 Nov. 1886
	Provincial boundary

0   250   500 miles

0   250   500 km

Atlantic Ocean

Hudson Bay

BRITISH
COLUMBIA
*1871 Joined
Dominion*

HUDSON'S BAY COMPANY
(Territory annexed to Dominion 1870)

NEWFOUNDLAND

Albany R.

QUEBEC
(Lower
Canada)

St. Lawrence

NEW
BRUNSWICK

*Separately
administered*

U N I T E D   S T A T E S

L. Superior

ONTARIO
(Upper Canada)

Ottawa R. Quebec

Ottawa

Montreal

NOVA SCOTIA

L. Michigan

L. Huron

Toronto *L. Ontario*

Erie

Ontario

*Prince Edward Island:
joined Dominion 1873*

118 THE INDIAN MUTINY, 1857

KASHMIR

Peshawar

PUNJAB
1848

Rohilkhand

Kumaon

T I B E T

BALUCHISTAN
1877

Bikaner

Delhi

BHUTAN

SIND
1843

Ajmer

ASSAM
1826

BIHAR

RAJPUTANA

Benares

Bundelkhand

BENGAL
1765

Dacca

Gujarat

Indore

CENTRAL
PROVINCES
1861

*Chandernagor
(French)*

BURMA
1886

*Diu
(Portuguese)*

Baroda

Nagpur

Calcutta

*Damão
(Portuguese)*

Berar

Arakan

Bombay

Mahrattas

NIZAM'S
DOMINIONS

Northern Circars

Cuttack

Hyderabad

Pegu
1852

Rangoon

Malabar

*Goa
(Portuguese)*

*Yanaon
(French)*

Karnatic

British possessions in 1763

British possessions acquired
between 1763 and 1815

MYSORE

Madras

British possessions acquired
between 1815 and 1856

*Mahé
(French)*

*Pondicherry
(French)*

Principal area of Indian Mutiny

*Karikal
(French)*

200   400 miles

CEYLON

200   400   600 km

119 EXPANSION OF INDUSTRY IN THE 19TH CENTURY
For navigations and canals, see map 104, and railways, map 11

Legend:
- ▲ Boots and shoes
- ⊞ Carpets
- ▤ Coal mining
- ⊡ Confectionery
- ⊠ Cotton
- ⊙ Dockyard
- ▲ Fishing port
- △ Hosiery
- ▲ Iron and steel
- ✳ Lace
- ● Linen
- ⊞ Railway engineering
- ⊡ Port
- ■ Shipbuilding (steamships)
- △ Potteries
- ◫ Tin
- ✛ Wool manufacture

0 ___ 50 miles
0 ___ 50 km

SHETLAND ISLANDS

60°

57°

ORKNEY ISLANDS

Atlantic Ocean

OUTER HEBRIDES

Stornoway

HARRIS

Spey R.

Don R.
Dee R.   Aberdeen

Forfar
Tay R.   Dundee   Arbroath

Clydebank

Helensburgh   Kirkcaldy
Greenock   Leith

Clyde   Edinburgh

Glasgow   Lanark

Ayr   Galashiels

Nith R.   Hawick

NORTHUMBERLAND

North Sea

Wallsend
Tyne R.   South Shields
Consett   Sunderland
Bishop   Durham
Auckland   West Hartlepool
Stockton   Redcar
Middlesbrough   Whitby

Belfast

Lisburn

Newry

Barrow-in-Furness

Irish Sea

1819 First steamship
arrives from Savannah

Halifax   York   Bridlington
Dewsbury
Leeds   Hull
Preston   Ouse R.
Bolton   Scunthorpe
Liverpool   Grimsby

Carrickmacross

Birkenhead   Sheffield

Holyhead   Manchester   Mansfield
Crewe   Burslem

IRELAND

Newcastle-under-Lyme   Nottingham
Stafford   Derby   Melton   Norwich   Yare
Dove R.   Mowbray   Great Yarmouth
Wolverhampton   Leicester   Lowesto
Corby
Bridgnorth   Kettering   Colchester
Kidderminster   Birmingham   Wellingborough

Limerick

Northampton
Wye R.   Avon

Witney   1825 First steamship
to Calcutta
Stroud   London   Thames

St. George's Channel

Milford Haven

Kinsale

Pembroke   Newport   Bristol   Sheerne
Port Talbot   Chatham
Cardiff   Trowbridge   Kennet   Wey R.
Avonmouth   Frome   Wilton   Folkestone
Honiton   Wilton
Exe R.   Southampton
Portsmouth

51°

Tamar R.   Axminster   Bridport
Plymouth
Camborne   Devonport   *English Channel*

9°   A   6°   B   3°   C   0°   D   3°

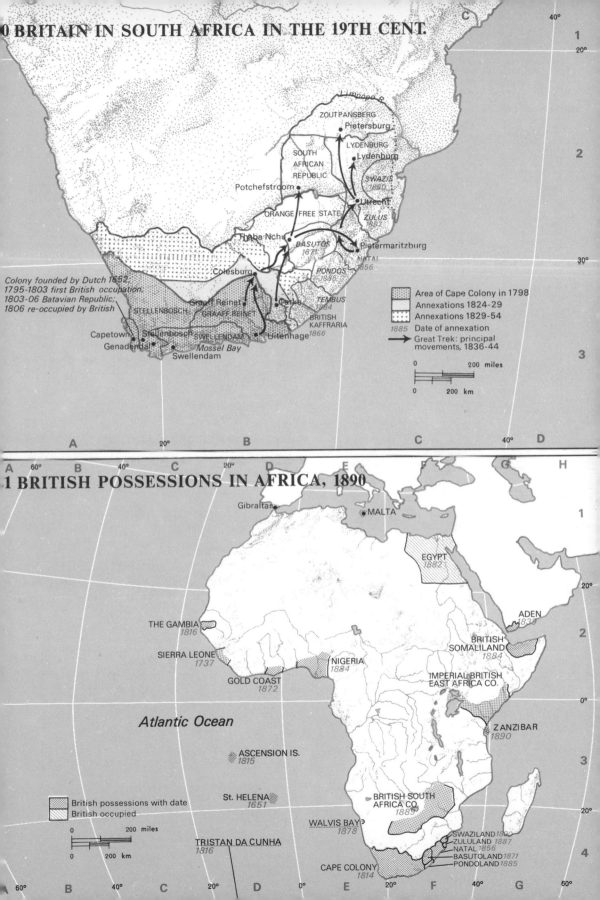

0 BRITAIN IN SOUTH AFRICA IN THE 19TH CENT.

Limpopo R.

ZOUTPANSBERG
Pietersburg

SOUTH
AFRICAN
REPUBLIC

LYDENBURG
Lydenburg

SWAZIS
1890

Potchefstroom

Utrecht

ORANGE FREE STATE

ZULUS
1887

Thaba Nchu

BASUTOS
1871

Pietermaritzburg

Colesburg

PONDOS
1886

NATAL
1856

Colony founded by Dutch 1652,
1795-1803 first British occupation,
1803-06 Batavian Republic,
1806 re-occupied by British

Graaff Reinet
GRAAFF REINET

Cradock

TEMBUS
1864

STELLENBOSCH

BRITISH
KAFFRARIA

Capetown
Genadendal

Stellenbosch

SWELLENDAM
Mossel Bay
Swellendam

Uitenhage
1866

	Area of Cape Colony in 1798
	Annexations 1824-29
	Annexations 1829-54
1885	Date of annexation
→	Great Trek: principal movements, 1836-44

0   200 miles

0   200 km

1 BRITISH POSSESSIONS IN AFRICA, 1890

Gibraltar

MALTA

EGYPT
1882

THE GAMBIA
1816

SIERRA LEONE
1737

NIGERIA
1884

GOLD COAST
1872

ADEN
1839

BRITISH
SOMALILAND
1884

IMPERIAL BRITISH
EAST AFRICA CO.

Atlantic Ocean

ASCENSION IS.
1815

ZANZIBAR
1890

St. HELENA
1651

| | British possessions with date |
| | British occupied |

0   200 miles

0   200 km

TRISTAN DA CUNHA
1816

BRITISH SOUTH
AFRICA CO.
1889

WALVIS BAY
1878

SWAZILAND *1890*
ZULULAND *1887*
NATAL *1856*
BASUTOLAND *1871*
PONDOLAND *1885*

CAPE COLONY
1814

122 LOCAL GOVERNMENT REFORM, 1888-98

The Local Government Act, 1888, instituted
Urban and Rural Districts, which could
only be shown on a very large map.
The Welsh Counties are those of 1836.
Scottish and Irish Counties are those of
the Acts of Union of 1707 and 1802

English Counties

1. Bedfordshire
2. Berkshire
3. Buckinghamshire
4. Cambridgeshire
5. Cheshire
6. Cornwall (inc. Scilly Is.)
7. Cumberland
8. Derbyshire
9. Devonshire
10. Dorsetshire
11. Durham
12. Essex
13. Gloucestershire
14. Hampshire
15. Herefordshire
16. Hertfordshire
17. Huntingdonshire
18. Kent
19. Lancashire
20. Leicestershire
21. Lincolnshire
22. London
23. Middlesex
24. Norfolk
25. Northamptonshire
26. Northumberland
27. Nottinghamshire
28. Oxfordshire
29. Rutland
30. Shropshire
31. Somerset
32. Staffordshire
   Suffolk
33. West Suffolk
34. East Suffolk
35. Surrey
   Sussex
36. West Sussex
37. East Sussex
38. Warwickshire
39. Westmorland
40. Wiltshire
41. Worcestershire
   Yorkshire
42. East Riding
43. North Riding
44. West Riding

Welsh Counties

45. Anglesey
46. Brecknock
47. Cardigan
48. Carmarthen
49. Caernarvon
50. Denbigh
51. Flint
52. Glamorgan
53. Merioneth
54. Monmouthshire
55. Montgomery
56. Pembroke
57. Radnor

Irish Counties

58. Antrim
59. Armagh
60. Carlow
61. Clare
62. Cavan
63. Cork
64. Down
65. Dublin
66. Fermanagh
67. Galway
68. Kerry
69. Kildare
70. Kilkenny
71. Laoghis
72. Leitrim
73. Limerick
74. Londonderry
75. Longford
76. Louth
77. Mayo
78. Meath
79. Monaghan
80. Offaly
81. Roscommon
82. Sligo
83. Tipperary
84. Donegal
85. Tyrone
86. Waterford
87. Westmeath
88. Wexford
89. Wicklow

Scottish Counties

90. Aberdeen
91. Argyll
92. Ayr
93. Banff
94. Berwick
95. Bute
96. Caithness
97. Clackmannan
98. Dumfries
99. Dumbarton
100. East Lothian
101. Fife
102. Forfar
103. Inverness
104. Kincardine
105. Kinross
106. Kirkcudbright
107. Lanark
108. Midlothian
109. Moray
110. Nairn
111. Orkney Is.
112. Peebles
113. Perth
114. Renfrew
115. Ross and Cromarty
116. Roxburgh
117. Selkirk
118. Shetland Is.
119. Stirling
120. Sutherland
121. West Lothian
122. Wigtown

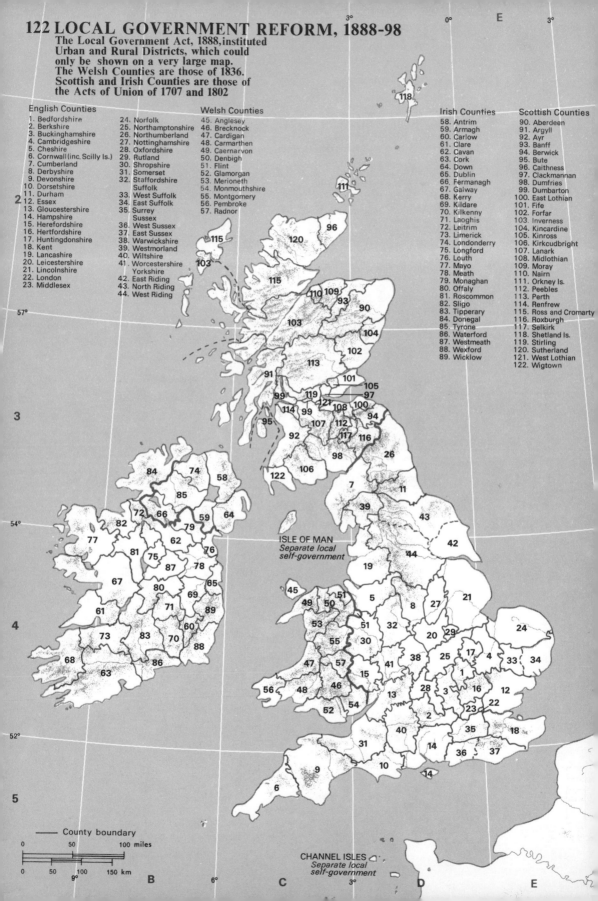

ISLE OF MAN
*Separate local
self-government*

— County boundary

0   50   100 miles

0 50 100 150 km

CHANNEL ISLES
*Separate local
self-government*

123 THE BOER WAR, 1899-1902

SOUTH AFRICAN REP.

17 May 1900
Siege lifted
Mafeking

Pretoria
5 June 1900
Machadodorp
Diamond Hill
11-12 June 1900
Dalmanutha
27 Aug. 1900

Doornkop

Johannesburg
31 May 1900

Vereeniging
Vaal R.

Volksrust

Talana Hill
20 Oct. 1899

Newcastle

ORANGE FREE STATE
Tweefontein
25 Dec. 1901
Vaal Krantz
5 Feb. 1900

Dundee

Elands Laagte
21 Oct. 1899

..eb. 1900
..ge lifted

Magersfontein

Brandwater

Ladysmith

Tugela R.

Paardeberg
27 Feb. 1900
Brandfort

Spion Kop
24 Jan. 1900

Colenso
15 Dec. 1899

..imberley

Bloemfontein
13 March 1900

N A T A L

..span

Sannah's Post
31 March 1900

Pietermaritzburg

Poplar Grove
Abraham's Kraal

Wepener

BASUTOLAND

Durban

Orange R.

De Aar

CAPE COLONY

DRAKENSBERG

Colesberg

Naauwpoort

Stormberg
10 Dec. 1899

NATIVE
TERRITORIES

● Captured by British (with date)
✗ British victory
⟶ British movement
✗ Boer victory
★ Besieged by Boers
⟶ Boer movement
Railway
Border

0   50   100 miles
0   50   100   150 km

Area of Boer War

SOUTHERN RHODESIA

PORTUGUESE EAST AFRICA

S. AFRICAN REPUBLIC

ORANGE FREE STATE

SWAZILAND

NATAL

CAPE COLONY

BASUTOLAND

NATIVE TERRITORIES

124 INDIA BEFORE PARTITION, 1906-47

Herat

Chitral
1895

KASHMIR
1846

Kabul

Peshawar

Srinagar

Charoba

AFGHANISTAN

Kandahar

N.W.F.P.

PUNJAB
1846

Lahore

Garhwal

T I B E T

Quetta

Multan

Simla
1876

BALUCHISTAN
1876

BAHAWALPUR
1838

Delhi

PATIALA

UNITED

NEPAL

SIKKIM
1816

Darjeeling

BHUTAN

Indus R.

RAJPUTANA
1818

Agra

PROVINCES

Bareilly

COOCH

ASSAM
1826

KHAIRPUR

SIND
1843

Karachi

SINDHIA
1800

Cawnpore

OF AGRA & OUDH
1856

Patna

BIHAR
1765

BENGAL
1765

MANIPUR

Upper Burma
1886

Cutch

Ajm..
1818

CENTRAL

I N D I A

Chota Nagpur

Chandernagor

Chittagong

Mandalay

Ahmadabad

Bhopal

PINDARIS
1818

Ganges R.

Calcutta
1690

KATHIAWAR
1817

Baroda

CENTRAL
PROVINCES
BHONSLA
1853

ORISSA
1803

BURMA

Diu

Surat

Berar
1853

BASTAR

Damão

Bombay
1662

HYDERABAD
NIZAM
1798

The Circars
1766

Rangoon

Satara
1848

Karenni

Goa
(Portuguese)

Madras
1639

MYSORE
1799

Bay of Bengal

Andaman Is.

Arabian Sea

Mahé

Pondicherry

Karikal

Port Blair

Tanjore

1853

Cochin

Travancore
1788

CEYLON
1802

Bangkok

Colombo

Direct British control
Under British administration
Indian Protected States
Separate Governor-General
Independent
1801   Date of acquisition or annexation
N.W.F.P. North-West Frontier Province

0   100   200 miles
0   100 200 km

125 THE FIRST WORLD WAR, 1914-18 EUROPE

GREAT BRITAIN

Scapa Flow

Battle of Jutland
31 May 1916, draw

Dogger Bank
24 Jan. 1915

NORWAY

SWEDEN

Copenhagen

DENMARK

Heligoland Bight
28 Aug. 1914

British naval raid on
German U-boat bases,
22-23 Apr. 1918
9-10 May 1918

London

20 Oct.-11 Nov. 1914
22 Apr.-24 May 1915
22 July-20 Nov. 1917

Ypres
Brussels
Liège
Namur
Mons
Cambrai
20 Nov. 1917
Verdun
21 Feb.-Dec. 1916

Battles of the Marne
5-11 Sept. 1914
15 July-2 Aug. 1918

Paris

Lux.
1914
Metz

FRANCE

RUSSIA

Riga
1918
1917

1918

Tannenberg
27 Aug. 1914
1914

Brest-Litovsk

Warsaw

Danzig

Berlin

GERMAN EMPIRE

Prague

Munich

SWITZERLAND
Berne

ITALY

CORSICA

SARDINIA

Vienna

AUSTRO-HUNGARIAN EMPIRE

Budapest

Battles of the Isonzo:
Italians win 1915, Italians
win 6th Battle of Isonzo,
reach Gorizia

Gorizia

Belgrade

1915

1915

1915

SERBIA

MONTE-NEGRO

ALBANIA

GREECE

Salonika

Allied troops 1915

Black Sea

29-30 Oct. 1914
Turkish fleet bombards
Russian ports

Sevastopol

Odessa

RUMANIA
Bucharest
6 Dec. 1916,
Bucharest falls
1916

BULGARIA
Sofia

Constantinople

Gallipoli

OTTOMAN EMPIRE

Legend

Central Powers

Occupied by Central
Powers, 1914-17

Allied Powers

Advance of Central
Powers; advance

Maximum limit of Central
Powers' advance

– – – The Hindenburg Line

········· Line of trench warfare

Line of Allied advance, 1918

✕ Battle site

British naval victory

British naval blockade

0   100   200 miles
0   100   200 km

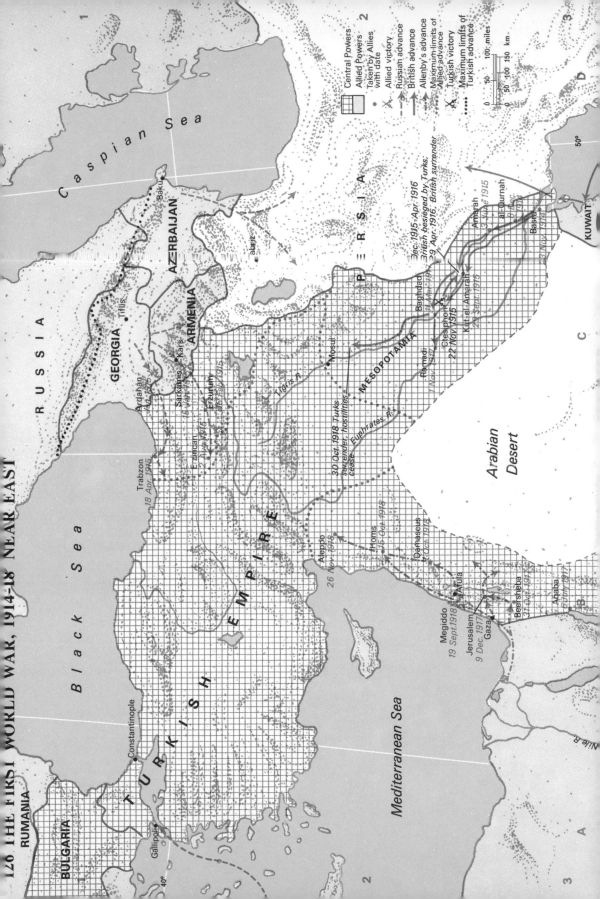

Legend:

Central Powers

Allied Powers

Taken by Allies with date

Allied victory

Russian advance

British advance

Allenby's advance

Maximum limits of Allied advance

Turkish victory

Maximum limits of Turkish advance

0 50 100 150 km

0 50 100 miles

RUMANIA

BULGARIA

Caspian Sea

Black Sea

RUSSIA

Baku

Tiflis

GEORGIA

AZERBAIJAN

ARMENIA

Ardahan
16 Apr. 1915

Sarkamis
16 Jan. 1915

Kars

Tabriz

P E R S I A

Erzurum
16 Feb. 1916

Erzincan
2 July 1916

Trabzon
18 Apr. 1916

Constantinople

Gallipoli

T U R K I S H   E M P I R E

Mosul

Tigris R.

Euphrates R.

MESOPOTAMIA

30 Oct. 1918 Turks surrender; hostilities cease

Ramadi
1 Nov. 1917

Baghdad
11 Mar. 1917

Ctesiphon
22 Nov. 1915

Kut el Amarah
29 Sept. 1915

Dec.1915-Apr.1916 British besieged by Turks; 29 Apr. 1916, British surrender

Amarah
3 June 1915

al Qurnah
9 Dec. 1914

Basra
21 Nov. 1914

KUWAIT

50°

Arabian Desert

Aleppo
26 Nov. 1918

Homs
16 Oct. 1918

Damascus
1 Oct. 1918

Afula

Megiddo
19 Sept.1918

Jerusalem
9 Dec. 1917

Gaza
31 Oct. 1917

Beersheba
31 Oct. 1917

Aqaba
6 Jul. 1917

Mediterranean Sea

Nile R.

40°

127 THE PARTITION OF IRELAND, 1922

Following Government of Ireland Act,
1920 and treaty of 6 Dec. 1921.
First Northern Ireland Parliament met
5 June 1921; name of Irish Free State
agreed by Dail 7 Jan. 1922; became
Republic of Ireland 29 Dec. 1937

Londonderry
LONDONDERRY
ANTRIM
DONEGAL
TYRONE
Belfast
NORTHERN IRELAND
ULSTER
Armagh
FERMANAGH
ARMAGH
Sligo
LEITRIM
MONAGHAN
SLIGO
CAVAN
LOUTH
MAYO
Irish Sea
Knock
ROSCOMMON
LONGFORD
MEATH
CONNAUGHT
WESTMEATH
GALWAY
IRISH FREE STATE
Maynooth
Dublin
(Kilmainham)
Galway
OFFALY
KILDARE
DUBLIN
The Curragh
LEINSTER
WICKLOW
LEIX
CLARE
CARLOW
Ennis
KILKENNY
TIPPERARY
Vinegar Hill
LIMERICK
WEXFORD
MUNSTER
Wexford
Rosslare
KERRY
Waterford
Killarney
WATERFORD
CORK
Cork

Northern Ireland boundary
Provincial boundary
County boundary

0   20   40   miles
0   20   40   60 km

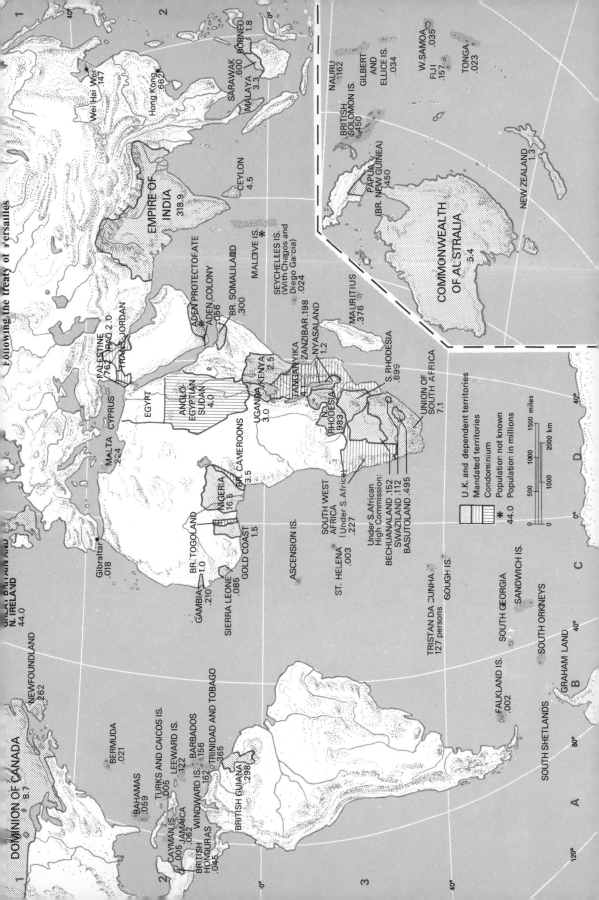

Following the Treaty of Versailles

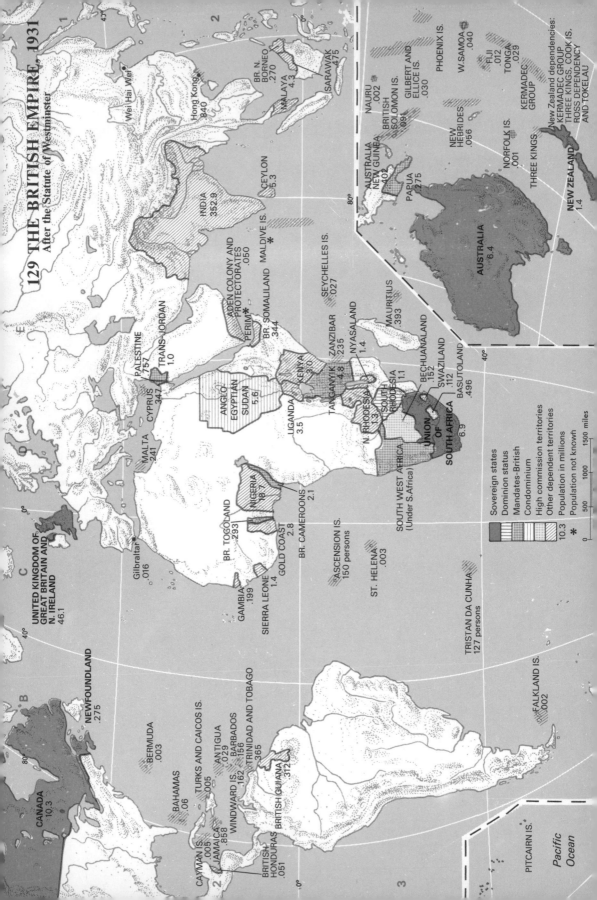

129 THE BRITISH EMPIRE, 1931
After the Statute of Westminster

UNITED KINGDOM OF GREAT BRITAIN AND N. IRELAND 46.1

NEWFOUNDLAND .275

CANADA 10.3

BERMUDA .003

BAHAMAS .06

CAYMAN IS. .005

JAMAICA .858

TURKS AND CAICOS IS. .005

ANTIGUA .029

WINDWARD IS. .162

BARBADOS .156

TRINIDAD AND TOBAGO .365

BRITISH HONDURAS .051

BRITISH GUIANA .312

FALKLAND IS. .002

PITCAIRN IS. *

Pacific Ocean

Gibraltar .016

MALTA .241

CYPRUS .347

PALESTINE .757

TRANS-JORDAN 1.0

ANGLO EGYPTIAN SUDAN 5.6

ADEN COLONY AND PROTECTORATES .050

PERIM*

BR. SOMALILAND .344

MALDIVE IS. *

NIGERIA 18.7

BR. TOGOLAND .293

GOLD COAST 2.8

BR. CAMEROONS 2.1

GAMBIA .199

SIERRA LEONE 1.4

ASCENSION IS. 150 persons

ST. HELENA .003

TRISTAN DA CUNHA 127 persons

UGANDA 3.5

KENYA 3.0

TANGANYIKA 4.8

ZANZIBAR .235

NYASALAND 1.4

N. RHODESIA 1.3

S. RHODESIA 1.1

BECHUANALAND .152

SWAZILAND .112

BASUTOLAND .496

SOUTH WEST AFRICA (Under S.Africa)

UNION OF SOUTH AFRICA 6.9

SEYCHELLES IS. .027

MAURITIUS .393

INDIA 352.9

CEYLON 5.3

Wei Hai Wei

Hong Kong .840

BR. N. BORNEO .270

MALAYA 4.3

SARAWAK .475

NAURU .002

AUSTRALIAN NEW GUINEA .402

BRITISH SOLOMON IS. .091

PAPUA .275

NEW HEBRIDES .056

NORFOLK IS. .001

THREE KINGS

PHOENIX IS.

W.SAMOA .040

FIJI .012

TONGA .029

KERMADEC GROUP

GILBERT AND ELLICE IS. .030

NEW ZEALAND 1.4

AUSTRALIA 6.4

New Zealand dependencies: KERMADEC GROUP THREE KINGS, COOK IS. ROSS DEPENDENCY AND TOKELAU

Sovereign states

Dominion status

Mandates-British

Condominium

High commission territories

Other dependent territories

Population in millions 10.3

* Population not known

DEFEAT AND VICTORY IN EUROPE, 1939-40

England and the Allies

Allied movements

Russian movements following the Russo-German Pact, 1939

Axis Powers, 1939

German advance

Occupied areas by 1940

German border, 1942

Maginot Line

German bombing missions

200 miles

300 km

UNION OF SOVIET SOCIALIST REPUBLICS

Black Sea

30 Nov. 1939 Russian invasion of Finland

March 1940 Area ceded to Soviet Union

10 Oct. 1939 Estonia, Latvia, Lithuania admit Soviet troops

17 Sept. 1939 Russian invasion of Poland

FINLAND

ESTONIA

LATVIA

LITHUANIA

EAST PRUSSIA

POLAND

Warsaw

Kutno

Kelce

Lvov

Modava

SLOVAKIA

RUMANIA

Bucharest

BULGARIA

Sofia

YUGOSLAVIA

Belgrade

Sarajevo

ALBANIA

GREECE

28 Oct. 1940 Unsuccessful Italian invasion of Greece

TURKEY

SWEDEN

Oslo

Trondheim

Bergen

Stavanger

Kristiansand

NORWAY

To Narvik

To Narvik

May-June 1940 British invade Norway

1940 Allied landings in Norway

9 Apr. 1940 German invasion of Norway and Denmark

DENMARK

Copenhagen

GERMANY

Berlin

1 Sept. 1939 German invasion of Poland

Prague

BOHEMIA-MORAVIA

SUDETEN

Munich

AUSTRIA

Budapest

HUNGARY

SWITZ.

Mainz

10 May-26 June 1940 German invasion of France

Wesermünde

NETHERLANDS

Rotterdam

Brussels

BELGIUM

10-28 May 1940

5 June 1940 (15 May 1940)

Dunkirk

3 June 1940 Evacuated

Amiens

Sedan

Paris

Dijon

Vichy

'Unoccupied France'

Tours

Rennes

ITALY

Rome

Entered war 1940

CORSICA

SARDINIA

GREAT BRITAIN

N. IRELAND

EIRE

London

28 June 1940 General de Gaulle recognized as head of French resistance

8 Aug.-5 Oct. Battle of Britain over southern England: R.A.F. defeats German Air Force

Atlantic Ocean

SPAIN

Madrid

PORTUGAL

Lisbon

131 THE MIDDLE EASTERN THEATRE, 1939-43

SPAIN
PORTUGAL
GREECE
TURKEY
ITALY
Tangier
Oran
Algiers
Bone
Bizerta
Tunis
MALTA
Sept. 1943 Allied invasion of Italy
SYRIA 1941
IRAQ 1941
IRAN
Casablanca
Tebessa
Gafsa
Sfax
Gabes
Tripoli
TUNISIA
Mareth Line
CYPRUS
LEBANON 1941
Baghdad
Habbaniyah
12 May 1943 Germans surrender in North Africa
MOROCCO
Gazala
Derna
Tobruk
Bardia
Sidi Barrani
El Alamein
Cairo
Damascus
PALESTINE
TRANSJORDAN
Basra
Benghazi
Agedabia
El Agheila
ALGERIA
LIBYA
EGYPT

Italy and annexed territory, 1940
British territory in Africa, 1940
VIIIth Army's advance, 1940-43
Ist Army's advance, 1942-43
German (Rommel) advance, 1941-42
1940 British takeover
Swamp area

Sahara Desert

FRENCH WEST AFRICA
ANGLO-EGYPTIAN SUDAN
ERITREA
YEMEN
17 March 1940 B. take Berbera
FRENCH EQUATORIAL AFRICA
NIGERIA
Jan. 1940
FRENCH SOMALILAND
Aden
BRITISH SOMALILAND
Berbera
4-17 Aug. Taken by It.
BRITISH TOGOLAND
GOLD COAST
FRENCH TOGOLAND
FRENCH CAMEROUN
BRITISH CAMEROONS
20 Jan. 1941 Emperor Haile Selassie restored 5 Apr. Addis Ababa taken from Italians
Addis Ababa
ETHIOPIA
ITALIAN SOMALILAND
Mogadis

0   500   1000 miles
0   500   1000 km
0°

BELGIAN CONGO
UGANDA
KENYA

132 THE FAR EASTERN THEATRE, 1941-45

ALASKA
CANA
U. S. S. R.
MONGOLIA
Aug. 1942
ATTU
ALEUTIAN IS.
KISKA
Dutch Harbour 3 June 1942
May 1942
MANCHUKUO
Jehol
Aug.
KURIL IS.
UNIT STAT
CHINA
Hiroshima 6 Aug.
Tokyo
Nagasaki 9 Aug. '45
18 Apr. 1942
TIBET
Shanghai
Apr.-2 July 1945
JAPAN
IWOJIMA 19 Feb.-16 Mar. 1945
MIDWAY
Battle of Midway 3-6 June 1942
NEPAL
1945
TAIWAN
OKINAWA
Feb. '45
INDIA
Hong Kong 8 Dec. 1941
WAKE IS. 8 Dec. 1941
HAWAII
Pearl Harbour 7 Dec. 1941
INDO-CHINA
8 Dec. 1941
MARIANA IS.
SAIPAN
JOHNSTON
Rangoon
SIAM
10 Dec. 1941
Manila
PHILIPPINES
GUAM
June 1944
ANDAMAN IS.
Bangkok
3 Mar. 1945
Leyte Gulf 23-25 Oct. 1944
Battle of Philippine Sea 19 June 1944
ENINETOK
MARSHALL IS.
Jan. 1944
PALAU
Sept. 1944
Oct. 1944
BRUNEI
MOROTAI
TURK
Nov. 1943
SUMATRA
Singapore
BORNEO
GILBERT AND ELLICE IS.
Allies   Japanese
Territory held 194
Advance
Victory
Bombing mission
Atom Bomb atta
Maximum limit o Japanese conqu 1942
Hollandia
NEW GUINEA
PAPUA
Rabaul
SOLOMON
JAVA
Battle of Java Sea 27 Feb. 1942
TIMOR
Port Darwin
Guadalcanal 7 Aug. 1942-7 Feb. 1943
Battle of Coral Sea 5-8 May 1942
Aug. '42
NEW HEBRIDES
FIJI IS.
0   1000   2000 miles
0   1000   2000 km
AUSTRALIA

THE VICTORY IN EUROPE, 1943-45

Allied advance:
1943
1944
1945
German defence line
Maximum German advance
German area, May 1945

0   100   200 miles
0   100   200   300 km

Leningrad
Kalinin
Moscow
Yelets
Voronezh
Stalingrad
Rostov
Stalino
Taganrog
Belgorod
Kharkov
Kursk
Orel
Bryansk
Smolensk
Roslavl
Bobruysk
Sholobin
Zhitomir
Kiev
Berdichev
Cherkassy
Kremenchug
Dnepr
Sevastopol
Odessa
Donets
Don
Galati
Iasi
Tiraspol
Craiova
Bucharest
Sofia
Nis
Giurgiu
Sibiu
Cluj
Arad
Timisoara
Belgrade
Szeged
Vac
Budapest
Pskov
Narva
Revel
Riga
Tukums
Polotsk
Vitebsk
Minsk
Vilna
Kovno
Konigsberg
Grodno
Memel
Danzig
Bialystok
Pultusk
Pinsk
Brest-Litovsk
Kovel
Lvov
Sandomierz
Lublin
Krakow
Warsaw
Poznan
Breslau
Gorlitz
Glogau
Kustrin
Frankfurt
Hamburg
Bremen
Berlin
Magdeburg
Dessau
Dresden
Chemnitz
Prague
Pilsen
Brunn
Wels
Radboz.
Linz
Salzburg
St. Polten
Vienna
Brenner Pass
Gorizia
Trieste
Bologna
Florence
Spezia
Livorno
Genoa
Milan
Como
Rome
Anzio
Naples
Salerno
Foggia
Taranto
Messina
Catania
Gela
PANTELLERIA
MALTA
Tunis
Oran
Madrid
Lisbon
Munich
Stuttgart
Mannheim
Mainz
Coblenz
Wesel
Arnhem
Aix
Antwerp
WALCHEREN
London
Ipswich
Southampton
Brighton
Weymouth
Plymouth
Falmouth
Brest
Lorient
Nantes
Le Mans
Avranches
Cherbourg
Carentan
Caen
Falaise
Argentan
Rouen
Paris
Reims
Orleans
Metz
Strasbourg
Besancon
Dijon
Vichy
Lyons
Grenoble
Marseilles
Toulon
30°
20°
30°
40°
40°
50°
2
3
4
F
E
D
C
B
2
3
4

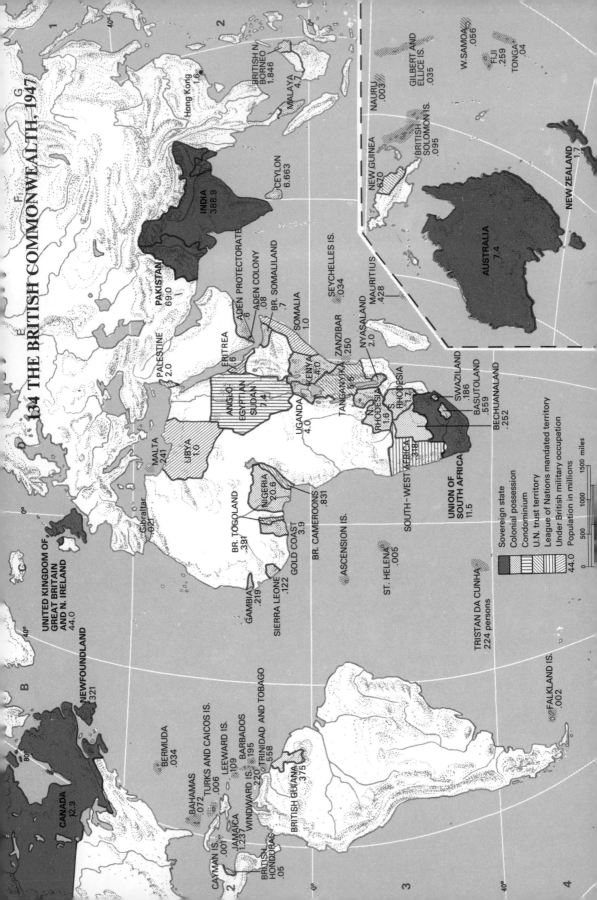

134 THE BRITISH COMMONWEALTH, 1947

UNITED KINGDOM OF GREAT BRITAIN AND N. IRELAND
44.0

NEWFOUNDLAND
.321

CANADA
12.3

BERMUDA
.034

BAHAMAS
.072

TURKS AND CAICOS IS.
.006

CAYMAN IS.
.001

JAMAICA
1.237

LEEWARD IS.
.109

WINDWARD IS.
.220

BARBADOS
.195

TRINIDAD AND TOBAGO
.558

BRITISH HONDURAS
.05

BRITISH GUIANA
.375

FALKLAND IS.
.002

TRISTAN DA CUNHA
224 persons

ST. HELENA
.005

ASCENSION IS.

GAMBIA
.219

SIERRA LEONE
.122

BR. TOGOLAND
.391

GOLD COAST
3.9

NIGERIA
20.6

BR. CAMEROONS
.831

Gibraltar
.021

MALTA
.241

LIBYA
1.0

ANGLO EGYPTIAN SUDAN
7.4

PALESTINE
2.0

ERITREA
.6

ADEN PROTECTORATE

ADEN COLONY
.08

BR. SOMALILAND
.7

SOMALIA
1.0

UGANDA
4.0

KENYA
4.0

ZANZIBAR
.250

SEYCHELLES IS.
.034

TANGANYIKA
5.5

NYASALAND
2.0

MAURITIUS
.428

RHODESIA
1.6

RHODESIA
1.7

SWAZILAND
.186

BASUTOLAND
.559

BECHUANALAND
.252

SOUTH-WEST AFRICA
.318

UNION OF SOUTH AFRICA
11.5

Hong Kong
1.6

BRITISH N. BORNEO
1.846

MALAYA
4.7

INDIA
388.9

PAKISTAN
69.0

CEYLON
6.663

NAURU
.003

NEW GUINEA
.670

BRITISH SOLOMON IS.
.095

GILBERT AND ELLICE IS.
.035

W. SAMOA
.056

FIJI
.259

TONGA
.04

NEW ZEALAND
1.7

AUSTRALIA
7.4

- Sovereign state
- Colonial possession
- Condominium
- U.N. trust territory
- League of Nations mandated territory
- Under British military occupation
- Population in millions 44.0

0   500   1000   1500 miles

135 BRITISH INDUSTRY IN THE 20TH CENT.

Legend:
- Oil field
- Gas field
- Limit of Sector
- Oil pipeline
- Gas pipeline
- Proposed gas pipeline
- Oil refining
- Petrochemicals
- Chemicals
- Nuclear power station
- Hydro-electric station
- Shipbuilding
- Motor manufacture
- Iron and steel
- Coal
- Woollen manufacture
- Man-made fibre
- Fishing port
- Civil airport
- Carpets
- Linen
- Jute
- Cotton

Dairying, rearing and grazing
Mixed farming
Mainly arable
Market gardening
Hill farming or heath
Crofting or subsistence farming
Urban area

0   50 miles
0   50 km

Map labels:

MAGNUS, THISTLE, MURCHISON, TERN, DUNLIN, STATFJORD, CORMORANT, HEATHER, BRENT, LYELL, HUTTON, NINIAN, ALWYN, FRIGG, BERYL, CRAWFORD, NORWEGIAN, BRAE, PIPER, TONI, CLAYMORE, THELMA, TARTAN, MAUREEN, ANDREW, BUCHAN, FORTIES, MONTROSE, LOMOND, EKOFISK, FULMAR, AUK, DANISH, ARGYLL, BRITISH, GERMAN, DUTCH

Lerwick, Kirkwall, Wick, Stornoway, BEATRICE, Peterhead, Cruden Bay, Aberdeen, Dundee, Edinburgh, Glasgow, Firth of Clyde

Londonderry, Belfast, Newcastle, Teesport, Barrow-in-Furness, ISLE OF MAN

Dublin, Wylfa, Liverpool, Birkenhead, Holyhead, Sheffield, Manchester, Stoke-on-Trent, Nottingham, Birmingham

ROUGH, WEST SOLE, AMETHYST, VIKING, BROKEN BANK, INDEFATIGABLE, DEBORAH, S.E. INDEFATIGABLE, HEWETT, LEMAN BANK, DOTTIE, Bacton, Great-Yarmouth, Lowestoft, Sizewell, Ipswich, Luton, Oxford, Coryton, London, Dungeness

Hull, Gloucester, Milford Haven, Swansea, Cardiff, Bristol, Exeter, Southampton, Bournemouth, CORFE CASTLE

Shannon, Whitegate, Cork, St. Just, St. Mary's, SCILLY IS.

FRENCH

136 LABOUR RELATIONS, 19TH TO 20TH CENTURY
(For county boundaries see map 140)

D   3°   E

- Principal unemployment, 1920 – 39
→ The 'Hunger March' in 1936, down Great North Road
1920's Strikes common (with date)
— Road

0   50   100 miles

0   50   100   150 km

SCOTLAND

NORTHUMBERLAND
1840 County Union formed
1844 Miners strike
1910 Miners strike

Clydeside
1915, strikes

Stirling   Kirkcaldy
Falkirk   Dunfermline

Glasgow
Early 1930's

New Lanark
*1820 ff. R. Owen's
'Model Mills'*

*1874 Engineers strike
successfully for 9 hour day*

Tyneside
*1910 Railway strike;
Boilermakers strike*

*Early 1920's;
late 1930's*

Morpeth
Newcastle Jarrow
Carlisle   *Tyne* Sunderland
          Consett Durham
Workington   Hartlepool
Whitehaven Bishop Teeside
          Auckland

1840 County Union formed
1844 Miners strike
1910 Miners strike

YORKSHIRE
1840 County Union formed

1859 Weavers strike

Bradford
Burnley
Leeds
Wakefield

1831 First Trade Union formed
1839 Chartist Convention
1893 Miners strike-2 killed in riot

LANCASHIRE
1840 County Union founded
*Preston and Stockport,
1853 47,000 spinners strike*

Padiham
Preston
1930's Huddersfield
Manchester   Barnsley
Liverpool   Stockport Rotherham
1930's   Sheffield
          Stoke-on-Trent

Scunthorpe
1843 Miners' Association formed

Accrington
1911 Weavers strike

1866 'Sheffield Outrages'

1819 'Peterloo Massacre'
1828 'Old Mechanics' founded
*1830 National Association for
Protection of Labour founded*
1838 Chartist demonstration
*1839 Anti-Corn Law League
founded*
*1899 General Federation of
Trades Union founded*

*1911 Dockers
strike*

Birmingham
*1839 Chartist
Convention*
Coventry

NOTTINGHAMSHIRE
1811-1812 Luddites

STAFFORDSHIRE
1840 County Union formed

WALES

1901 Taff Vale Railway case

Llanelli   Merthyr   Ebbw Vale
        Tydfil   *1893 Miners strike*
Swansea
Port Talbot   Newport
      Cardiff   Bristol

London

Tonypandy
*1901 Miners
strike and riot*

1839 Riots
1920's

Southampton
*1911 Dockers' strike
becomes general*

Tolpuddle
*1834 'Martyrs'
(pardoned 1836)*

London:
1824-25 Combination Laws
*1851 Amalgamated Society
of Engineers founded*
*1852 First T.U. candidate
stands in Parliamentary
election*
1859-60 Builders strike
*1860 London Trades Council
formed*
*1869 Trades Union Congress
founded*
*1872 Factory Acts Reform
Association founded. Abp.
Manning supports Arch's Union*
*1874 10 working men stand
at election*
1885 First miner M.P.
1889 London Dock strike

*1890 Hyde Park Meeting,
4 May*
1906 Labour Party founded
*1911 Suffragette violence at
its peak. Dockers strike*
*1915 first Labour Ministers
join Coalition*
1918 57 Labour M.P.s elected
1918-19 London Police strikes
1922 142 Labour M.P.s elected
1923 191 Labour M.P.s elected
1924 Jan-Nov, Labour Government
*1926 4 May-12 May, General strike;
1st May-19 Nov., Miners strike*
*1929 288 Labour M.P.s elected:
Labour Government to 1931*
1940-45 Labour joins Coalition
1945-51 1964-70, 1973, Labour Governm

57°

51°

1

2

3

4

A   6°   B   3°   C   D

137 BRITISH UNIVERSITIES AND COPYRIGHT LIBRARIES, 1978

A   9°   B   6°   C   3°   D   0°   E

SCOTLAND

Aberdeen
1494

Dundee
1967

St. Andrew's
1410

Stirling
1964

Library of the
Faculty of Advocates

Edinburgh
1583

Heriot–Watt
1966

Strathclyde
1964

Glasgow
1451

Coleraine
1968

Ulster
1970

**NORTHERN
IRELAND**

Queen's
Belfast
1845, 1909

Newcastle upon Tyne
1963

Durham
1832

ENGLAND

*Constituents of
Queen's University:
Queen's, Belfast;
Queen's, Dublin;
Cork; Galway*

Lancaster
1964

York
1963

Hull
1954

Bradford
1966

Leeds
1904

Galway
1909

Queen's
1845

Dublin
1591

National Univ.
1909

Trinity College

Salford
1967

Manchester
1880

Sheffield
1905

Liverpool
1903

E I R E

Bangor

Keele
1962

Nottingham
1948

Loughborough
1966

Cork
1909

WALES

University of
Wales
1893

Aberystwyth

**National Library
of Wales**

Birmingham
1900

Aston
1966

Leicester
1957

East Anglia
1964

Warwick
1964

**Cambridge
University
Library**

Cambridge,
(unknown)

Lampeter
1822

Buckingham
1976

Open University
1969

Essex
1864

Bodleian Library

Oxford
(unknown)

Swansea

British Museum

Kent
1965

Cardiff

Bristol
1909

Reading
1926

Surrey
1966

Sussex
1961

Bath
1966

Southampton
1952

Exeter
1955

London *1836*
Brunel *1966*
City *1966*

57°

54°

51°

1

2

3

4

Leeds
1904   University with date of foundation
           Copyright library

0   50   100 miles

0   50   100   150 km

A   B   6°   C   D   E

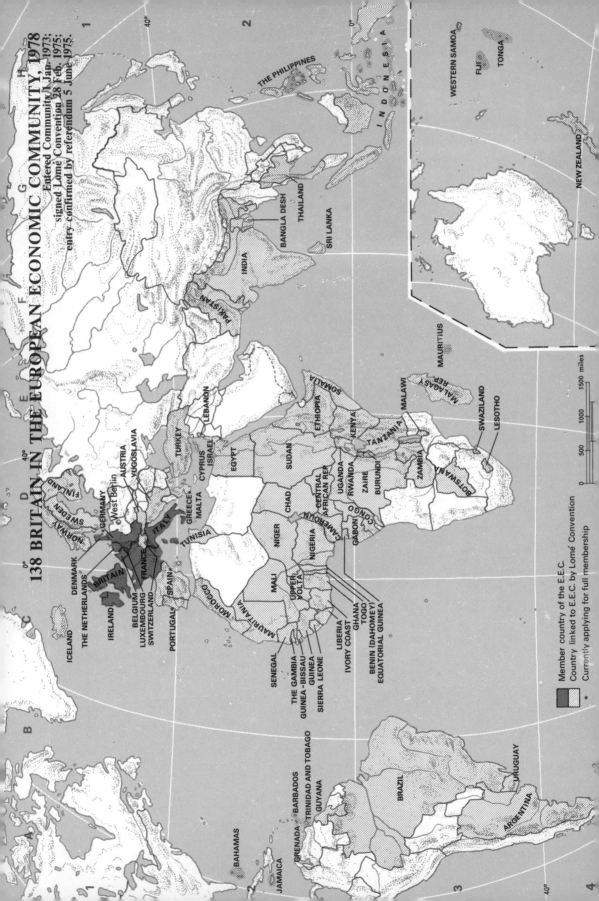

138 BRITAIN IN THE EUROPEAN ECONOMIC COMMUNITY, 1978

Entered Community 1 Jan. 1973;
signed Lomé Convention 28 Feb. 1975;
entry confirmed by referendum 5 June 1975.

Member country of the E.E.C.

Country linked to E.E.C. by Lomé Convention

* Currently applying for full membership

0   500   1000   1500 miles

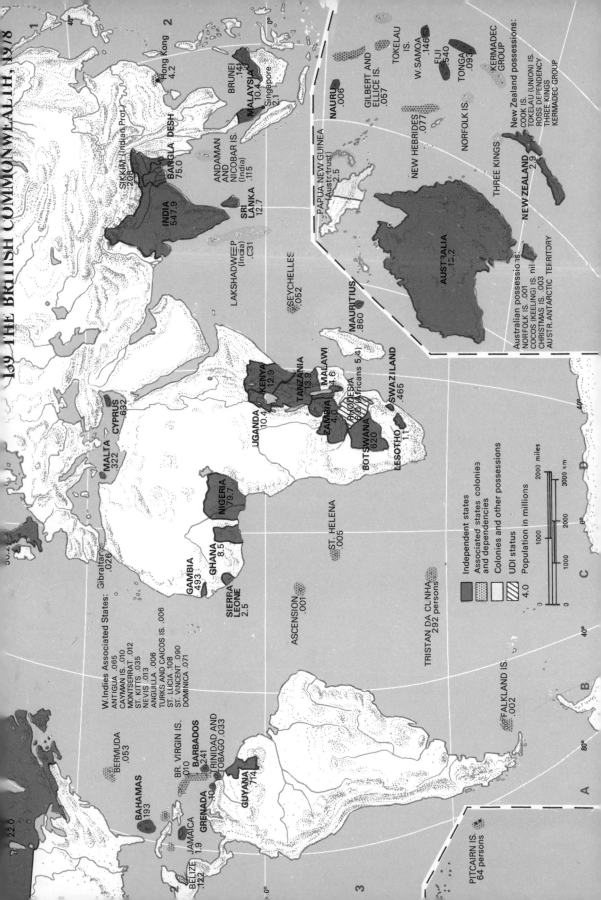

89 THE BRITISH COMMONWEALTH, 1978

Hong Kong 4.2

BRUNEI .141
MALAYSIA 10.4
Singapore 2.1

BANGLA- DESH 75.0
SIKKIM (Indian Prot.) .208
INDIA 547.9
ANDAMAN AND NICOBAR IS. (India) .115
SRI LANKA 12.7
LAKSHADWEEP (India) .031
SEYCHELLES .052

MALTA .322
CYPRUS .632
Gibraltar .026

GAMBIA .493
GHANA 8.5
SIERRA LEONE 2.5
NIGERIA 79.7
ST. HELENA .005
ASCENSION .001
TRISTAN DA CUNHA 292 persons

UGANDA 10.4
KENYA 12.9
TANZANIA 13.9
MALAWI 4.6
ZAMBIA 4.0
RHODESIA (Africans 5.4)
BOTSWANA .620
SWAZILAND .465
LESOTHO 1.1
MAURITIUS .860

BERMUDA .053
BAHAMAS .193
BR. VIRGIN IS. .010
JAMAICA 1.9
GRENADA .10
TRINIDAD AND TOBAGO .033
BARBADOS .241
BELIZE .132
GUYANA .714

W.Indies Associated States:
ANTIGUA .065
CAYMAN IS. .010
MONTSERRAT .012
ST. KITTS .035
NEVIS .013
ANGUILLA .006
TURKS AND CAICOS IS. .006
ST. LUCIA .108
ST. VINCENT .090
DOMINICA .071

FALKLAND IS. .002
PITCAIRN IS. 64 persons

NAURU .006
GILBERT AND ELLICE IS. .057
TOKELAU IS.
W.SAMOA .146
FIJI 540
TONGA .093
KERMADEC GROUP

PAPUA NEW GUINEA (Austr. trust) 2.5
NEW HEBRIDES .077
NORFOLK IS.
THREE KINGS
AUSTRALIA 12.2
NEW ZEALAND 2.9

New Zealand possessions:
COOK IS. .001
TOKELAU (UNION) IS.
ROSS DEPENDENCY
THREE KINGS
KERMADEC GROUP

Australian possession is:
NORFOLK IS. .001
COCOS (KEELING) IS. nil
CHRISTMAS IS. .003
AUSTR. ANTARCTIC TERRITORY

Independent states
Associated states colonies and dependencies
Colonies and other possessions
UDI status
4.0 Population in millions

0 1000 2000 3000 km
0 1000 2000 miles

140 ENGLISH, SCOTTISH AND WELSH COUNTIES AND REGIONS, 1978
Following the Local Government Act, 1972,
and the Local Government (Scotland) Act, 1973

Scotland
Regions
1. Highland
2. Grampian
3. Tayside
4. Fife
5. Lothian
6. Borders
7. Central
8. Strathclyde
9. Dumfries & Galloway

Islands Areas
10. Orkney
11. Shetland
12. Western Is.

England
13. Greater London

Metropolitan Counties
14. Greater Manchester
15. Merseyside
16. South Yorkshire
17. Tyne & Wear
18. West Midlands
19. West Yorkshire

Non-metropolitan Counties
20. Avon
21. Bedfordshire
22. Berkshire
23. Buckinghamshire
24. Cambridgeshire
25. Cheshire
26. Cleveland
27. Cornwall
28. Cumbria
29. Derbyshire
30. Devon
31. Dorset
32. Durham
33. East Sussex
34. Essex
35. Gloucestershire
36. Hampshire
37. Hereford & Worcester
38. Hertfordshire
39. Humberside
40. Isle of Wight
41. Kent
42. Lancashire
43. Leicestershire
44. Lincolnshire
45. Norfolk
46. North Yorkshire
47. Northhamptonshire
48. Northumberland
49. Nottinghamshire
50. Oxfordshire
51. Salop
52. Somerset
53. Staffordshire
54. Suffolk
55. Surrey
56. Warwickshire
57. West Sussex
58. Wiltshire

Wales
59. Clwyd
60. Dyfed
61. Gwent
62. Gwynedd
63. Mid Glamorgan
64. Powys
65. South Glamorgan
66. West Glamorgan

—— New boundary
—— Old boundary

0   50   100 miles
0 50 100 150 km

INDEX